SUCH DANCING AS WE CAN

SUCH DANCING AS WE CAN

SYDNEY LEA

The Humble Essayist
Press

The Humble Essayist Press
254 Butternut Creek Rd.
Blairsville, GA 30512

Copyright © 2023
Sydney Lea
All rights reserved
ISBN:
ISBN-13:

For my lockdown mate, now and forever, and in memory of Stephen Arkin

Be joyful though you have considered all the facts…
 —Wendell Berry.

Contents

Prologue: August 1

I. Sunya 2

The Cardinal, the Cops, and the Say-Hey Kid 3
Keepaway 15
Unholy 17
Forgiveness 20
Like Grant Took Richmond 22
Orange Order Fair, 1951 25
A Neighbor's Daydream 29
Familiar Stranger 34
Tough Luck 38
Unknown Saints 42
Fantasies in '56 45
1957 49
Mrs. Ragnetti and the Spider 55
Mentor 58
Battle of the Horns 61
Without Grace 63
Sixty Steps from Yale 65
Sunya 73

II. Bright Ambush 76

Earthquakes and Angels 77
Trail to Tomorrow 90
Short Sad Story 94
Bright Ambush 99

MICAH, WEEPING, 1978	101
AT MY AGE, I WHISTLE	103
STRANGER LOVE	107
THE COUPLE AT THE FREE PILE	109
SLOW ON THE UPTAKE	112
A STRANDED MOOSE	115
THEY SEEM TO KNOW	117
SAME OLD PATH:	120

III. SUNDAY MORNING 122

MY TRIBE AND I	123
REMORSE	152
ALL THINGS BRIGHT AND BEAUTIFUL	156
BLUES	160
ANOSMIA	163
STORYTELLING AT THE RES	167
STICKING TO FACTS	171
EVERYWHERE	174
TEMPORARY BACHELOR	176
ARMY SPECIALIZED DEPOT #829, 1942	179
NAKED TREES	182
BRIGHTER FOR ABSENCE	184
ONE MORE EULOGY	188
SUNDAY MORNING	191
NOVEMBER, 1981	195
THE KING OF JOKES	197
AMERICAN DREAM	203
IV. RAGE, IGNORANCE, LOVE	206
IN PRAISE OF IGNORANCE	207
RAVENS	209

vii

SHORT TREATISE ON SLOWING DOWN	211
IV. RAGE, IGNORANCE, LOVE	**216**
SUNDAY NOONS	223
WHAT TIME WAS IT?	226
SUPERNAL	228
MORE THAN FACT	230
HAZE	233
AFTER THE HEAT WAVE	236
THE WATER LOT	239
OKO	243
ON WEEPING	246
ABIDING BEAUTY	249
AFTER FIRST SNOW	252
REST AND BEAUTY	255
WHAT THE SMART PEOPLE THINK	258
REUNION	273
EPILOGUE: MATURITY	277
ACKNOWLEDGMENTS	287
STUDY GUIDE	289

Sydney Lea

Prologue: August

I'm blessed that in my corner of Vermont, I can literally step out our back door for a hike. I don't cross even a maintained dirt road, let alone any pavement, for a long, long time, and I walk on without seeing any dwellings, either, or none beyond the ones I mentally resurrect from their ancient cellar holes. I like doing that.

Unfortunately, much has interfered with my ramblings in recent years. In 2016, a tick-borne horror called ehrlichiosis stuck me in the hospital–including time in the ICU– and made me feel sicker than I ever have in an expansive life. It took me almost a year to get my energy back. Two knee replacements followed in successive years. And then came the COVID pandemic, during which I seemed until lately not to feel the usual hiking urge. I don't know why.

Yet my chief motive for staying out of the warm-weather woods derives from that enervating hospital stay. Although at my doctor's suggestion I keep two tablets of doxycycline on hand in case one of the horrid creatures embeds itself in my flesh again, I've remained deathly afraid of ticks ever since that ordeal.

But the proverbial elephant in my autobiographical room, of course, is that I'm now 80. This means, for instance, that I'll find myself looking for a stump-seat halfway up a ridge I used to charge and I'll wonder what on earth the problem can be. Yes, I used to *charge* up here! There's still an absurd interval before the light goes on: *Sure, you did that when you were fifty, even seventy... which you aren't anymore.* I fight to repress that awareness, but there it is.

I'm utterly undeserving of anyone's pity, I concede, least of all my own. I look around at so many friends who are lapsing into semi-incoherent senility, others who've been pushed even farther by Alzheimer's, and there's that mounting number of men and women who can't be seen at all. I'm a very lucky man: not only can I adore my life's partner, our five children, and all seven of our grandchildren, but I can also still bushwhack, if not with the same vigor, through the dense upper-New England woods, can paddle my canoe or kayak with some authority, what have you. And, in however stately a way, I can hike the hill trails.

Now for some, August is scarcely an ideal hiking month, especially now that with each passing year, the climate gets soggier and hotter. On the other hand, particularly in as dry a summer as the last one, those damned ticks are largely inert, and the vicious biting insects of earlier summer have pretty much gone too. At least at the month's beginning, the daylight hours linger long enough for me to go out early or else deep into the day, when some cool is available, to ramble around.

Needless to say, there are times Robert Frost's passage from "Birches" does apply:

> ...life is too much like a pathless wood
> Where your face burns and tickles with the cobwebs
> Broken across it, and one eye is weeping
> From a twig's having lashed across it open.

The spiders do start getting hyperactive at this time of year, and the trees and shrubs are so laden with foliage as to obscure clear vision now and then. I can trip and fall over invisible deadfalls and holes, and sure enough, an unseen twig will occasionally stab me somewhere.

But it is exactly the abundance of foliage that appeals to me. Under the unbroken canopy, I can feel –excuse the cliché– almost as if I'm back in the putative womb, protected and safe. Or I can all but imagine myself, despite the sweat, the abrasions, and the cobwebs, having been transported to some unearthly Eden.

This foolish delusion is temporary, as it should be. Everything is cyclical, and I know that in my very bones. Frost in the same poem immediately ponders such a matter:

Such Dancing as We Can

>   I'd like to get away from earth awhile
>   And then come back to it and begin over.
>   May no fate willfully misunderstand me
>   And half grant what I wish and snatch me away
>   Not to return. Earth's the right place for love:
>   I don't know where it's likely to go better.

Just as the in-the-womb coziness appeals, so can delivery *from* it. It's doubtless the imminence of fall and winter that starts me thinking that way. In any case, speaking for myself, that release enables me to celebrate the riches I possess, above all love, and more especially family love. Conscious as I become of their transience, I cherish all the crucial things even more deeply. As another poet, Wallace Stevens, asserted: "Death is the mother of beauty."

I have no notion what becomes of us after the Reaper does arrive, but every so often I get an odd little inkling of continuity, of everything's starting over, just as what we have contrived to call a year or four seasons has always done.

Here's a bizarre example. For the better part of a decade, I couldn't find my favorite pair of many boots. They're rugged enough, but they're made of the lightest leather possible. I'm scarcely alone in such frustration; the thing we seek must be right at hand, but *where?* One day as last

Sydney Lea

August waned, red maples in the wetlands beginning to show those heartbreak splashes of color, I found the boots in an unlikely closet, hidden behind boxes of my so-called papers. I let out a whoop, one loud enough to startle our three dogs. Then I sat down on a porch bench and slid my feet in, rejoicing at how perfectly the boots fit. Merely to wear them was to yearn for a hike.

I hadn't walked twenty feet, however, before I felt something uncomfortable under my right arch. I went back to the bench and removed the boot. A tiny acorn lay half-buried in the sole. It took a bit of effort to scrape it out, and when I did, rather than flicking it onto the grass, I unaccountably carried it between my thumb and forefinger out into the sunlight.

I took a quick and unexpected breath, in fact a gasp. As that gilded globe shimmered in the radiance, I reflected that it had made its way into my boot almost ten years back; that it had waited patiently for my foot to return; that it therefore should prompt me to take certain matters up where I'd left them.

I won't even try to sort out whether the tears occasioned by this small experience were ones of joy or melancholy, because they clearly involved both– and a whole lot more I'll never quite understand. I made for the woods.

I. Sunya

Sydney Lea

The Cardinal, the Cops, and the Say-Hey Kid

As I think my prologue implied, the woods I have referred to are as much metaphorical as literal; in these essays, indeed, they're often *more* so. To my mind, however, that's an impoverished distinction: I can get equally turned around (our northern New England euphemism for *lost*) in either thicket, and it's only by instinct and imagination that I make my way back to what we all, myself included, lazily name *reality,* as if the intervening ramble were not, as in my view it emphatically is, a reality of its own, the one that keeps a writer going.

One, anyhow.

I'm frequently asked how at my age I sustain the discipline to keep writing poetry and prose. Truth is, discipline has nothing to do with it. Writing is a way of knowing the world for which I have simply found no substitute; discipline is needed to *stop* writing, to understand the importance as well, say, of grocery shopping or cooking or, once upon a time, reading to our children or, now, their own children, at bedtime.

If I've maintained the writing habit for sixty years-plus, it's because I am addicted to discovering connections in my experience that I never knew were connections until I started tapping at my keys and then, to put matters a bit vaguely, I followed the lead of language. Rather than diminishing, the discoveries that crop up in the act of composition have become more thrilling, albeit stranger and stranger now that I have opened 80's door. I am astonished by the way some random observation can summon a skein of apparently unrelated memories. In some cases, to be sure, it does feel more like an explosion than a summons, when I am more unnerved than merely satisfied. But even such agitation has some ineffable value to me.

Here's a case in point. A few mornings ago, a cardinal flew into one of our windows. We heard the pop against the glass and went to inspect. There the lovely bird lay on new-fallen snow, the very emblem of *conspicuous*. I went out and picked up his corpse. Dislodged feathers lifted in the January wind, and blood dotted the white ground in an almost perfect circle around the body.

Swiftly, jarringly, and at first unaccountably, those brilliant smudges of blood swept me back seven decades. As my lifespan shortens, I am frequently rushed back over the decades, even when I don't especially want to be. The essays in this section of my book will indicate as much. The process is doubtless part of taking stock toward the end of a lucky life. *Where was I then?* I muse. *Where am I now?* How are *then* and *now* akin? How do they diverge?

Sydney Lea

It wasn't a winter day I recalled on seeing the scarlet bird, but one in June of 1951. I'd been tingling with excitement since the night before, because my father was taking me to my first major league baseball game. We'd be going courtesy of some friend I didn't know, a season ticketholder. Dad assured me this meant our spot in the stands would be better than almost anyone's. He also told me we'd see a rookie who, he predicted, would become a once-in-a-lifetime player. When I asked this star's name, he said "You'll find out soon enough."

I was intrigued. I mean, Dad had seen Babe Ruth play in his time! I didn't yet know much about the major leagues, but everyone– man, woman, fan, non-fan, kids big and little, *everyone!*– recognized the illustrious Bambino's name. Would this fellow outshine the Babe? Looking back, I think my father meant once in *my* lifetime.

He'd be right, as so often, bless him. But I get ahead of myself.

All the while Dad and I made our way to our gate at old Connie Mack Stadium, I vainly sought to disengage my hand from his. I wanted to look like more than a youngster. Five times a parent and seven a grandparent since then, I now completely understand his worry that I might get lost among the milling pedestrians.

Such Dancing as We Can

We were suddenly halted by a clot of them, some cheering as if they were already at the game. I could see nothing but a mass of bodies, but my tall dad observed what was going on, or rather *had* gone on. His grip got harder, painfully so, as he dragged me across the street and away from the gawkers.

Despite his strategy, from the far side of that small crowd I could turn and see a black man lying stone-still on the sidewalk, his blood bright against the gray of its concrete. Two cops, one short and pot-bellied, the other more than six feet and slim as a wand, loomed over him, each fondling a night stick and each, it appeared, half-smiling. The fallen man's face, however improbably, looked as peaceful as a sleeping person's. The whole scene completely bewildered and, to euphemize, unsettled me; it has also stayed with me since, even though my look at it was so fleeting.

I importuned my father: "What happened? What did that guy *do?*" He answered tersely: "I can't say, son. Could be anything." Then, his face showing an expression I'd never seen in all my brief time on earth, he added, "or nothing."

"But why," I asked, "would they beat him up for *nothing?*" Dad just pulled me along even faster.

"*Why?*" I insisted. Silence.

Sydney Lea

A whole lot makes grim sense to me now that didn't when I was so young and guileless. The second great war had ended a mere six years before, and while this was an eternity to a small child, it was an eyeblink to my father, who had commanded a company of so-called Colored Troops during that epical conflict. Though probably eight out of ten Americans today don't realize as much, it was not until 1948 that President Truman desegregated U.S. armed forces by executive order.

My father rarely mentioned his time in military service, and at such rare moments as he did, it was generally to tell us some funny anecdote. It was therefore my mother who much later told a story that was anything but amusing, and that actually accounted for my being born in Pennsylvania.

Before their transfer to Wales a year and some later and ultimately to Normandy, my dad's unit, all African-American save the commissioned officers, had been stationed in Gadsden, Alabama, the very heart of Jim Crow Dixie. It was my father's conviction, she said, and local customs be damned, that if he wanted to invite one or more of his soldiers into his Gadsden house, well, he would simply do it. Local customs, as it turned out, involved burning a cross on the lawn of anyone who entertained such an unacceptable notion.

Such Dancing as We Can

All but immediately after that incident, my mother chose to flee north to have me. her firstborn. The night before she took the northbound train, however, she woke her husband in the wee hours, convinced she'd heard the sound of a human being in torment outside. Dad, having circled the base with a flashlight and spoken to a sentry, concluded she'd imagined the noise, rattled as she was by the cross-burning. He went back to sleep. She didn't.

On that Sunday afternoon in June about a decade later, three years after Jackie Robinson broke the color barrier in major league baseball, we finally arrived at our entry into Connie Mack Stadium. A short man who chewed a dead cigar took our tickets and, annoyingly, tousled my hair. We were in.

I have a number of stunning memories from that day, the first of which I have described. Others, thank God, are for the most part less grotesque. I can still distinctly picture what I beheld once we emerged from the concrete tunnel: an awesome expanse of green. I remember it literally made me catch my breath. It seemed almost impossible to me that anyone would besmirch that huge, pristine span of grass by playing a game on it. But for all of that, there were busy human figures out there.

Once we'd found our seats, perhaps five rows back from the home team Phillies' dugout, my father whispered:

Sydney Lea

"That's a guy to watch." He pointed to a man, notable as one of three black Giants, who was shagging fungo flies in center field. He did not say that Giant was *the* guy to watch, just *a* guy.

"Why watch *him*?" I asked. Was that the star Dad had hinted at? I supposed so but wasn't quite sure.

"Why him?" I repeated.

"You'll see," he replied.

I was curious, to be sure, but also sufficiently entranced by the vista that I didn't even feel impatient for play to begin. By and by, of course, the players did come off the field and into their dugouts until the P.A. announcer read off the names of the starters for both teams. As the Giants players were introduced and stepped out to face the crowd, the hometown fans booed. That seemed understandable; these were our opponents, after all. But I got confused when, at the words *Willie Mays,* the jeering got notably louder.

I looked over at my father, who shook his head, if just perceptibly.

Mays batted third in the order. After both preceding hitters grounded out, he sent a single over the second base bag. The hit didn't seem especially impressive. But when the cleanup man stepped into the box– as with so many on both sides, I don't recall his name– Willie took what looked like a perilous lead off first. I do remember that Russ Myer pitched for the Phillies that afternoon, and that three times he tried a pickoff, Willie scooting back to the bag without even sliding.

On Myer's first delivery home, however, Mays lit out, making the second-base bag yards ahead of catcher Andy Seminick's throw and popping to his feet with a broad smile on his face. Even at nine, I could somehow discern glee in this man's expression, not mockery. He was having fun! Willie took an equally daring lead toward third, but the Giants' cleanup hitter popped harmlessly to the first baseman and the top half of the first inning was over.

"Boy, he's fast," I remarked. My father only smiled.

The Phillies' first batter walked, but the two following were uneventfully retired. Then Del Ennis scorched a line drive, and a loud cheer erupted all around us– until the center fielder chased it down, almost casually snaring the potential hit with one hand. Mays's put-out induced an eerie quiet from the stands.

Sydney Lea

In Mays's second at-bat, I watched his homer clear the opposite field wall, and in one of the later innings, I saw him lay down a perfect sacrifice bunt. Clearly, he could do about anything he wanted.

What I particularly recall but can't quite render in words is that, despite his very recent arrival to the big leagues, whenever this player came to the plate or stood on base or made for a fly ball, the atmosphere in the stadium was instantly, and as I say indescribably, changed, anticipation hanging in the air as thick as the cigarette smoke all around us. Despite the occasional vile shout from Phillies fans, including the unforgivable N-word, there was just something irrepressible about this player's manner. I felt sure no amount of boorishness could ever quash it.

I have some fancy terms in my old age that I did not command then, ones like *dynamism, verve, elan.* Any and all would have applied to this amazing athlete, who, in the bottom of the ninth, threw a strike to the plate from deep left center to nab a potentially tying baserunner and end the contest into the bargain.

The game over, we stood to exit the park. I looked up at my father, ready to state the obvious, that here was a person whose capacities and character were unmatched by any I'd ever witnessed.

Such Dancing as We Can

I didn't get the chance. Seeing my expression, he simply said, "I told you….and he'll be getting even better."

In the later years of this demigod's 22 in the majors, it would pain me to watch him on television. Most of his supernal skills evaporated, he now and then actually bumbled around in the outfield at Shea. In my late twenties by then, I would literally close my eyes when he took a feeble swing at a breaking ball or failed to chase down a fly or stood a mere foot or two off first if he did happen to get there. I didn't want to know him after his prime, didn't want to blemish that earliest of sporting memories. To this day wish I hadn't.

During that game in 1951, I'd been more or less distracted from the sight of the man the cops had knocked to the ground, but I think I know now why my father led us back to the parking lot by a circuitous route. No doubt the police were gone– who knew what had happened to their victim?– so I'd bet he worried some bloodstains might remain on street or sidewalk. I never asked.

I skip ahead to another Sunday, this one in 1965. I was a year out of college and, like so many, I watched TV footage from the state my mother had fled when she was eight months pregnant, the very one in which the great Willie Mays was born. Combat-geared white officers, with their dogs, their clubs, and their hoses, were attacking peaceful demonstrators as they crossed a bridge in Selma. Bodies lay inert on the pavement as the phalanx of police made its brutal way through the throng.

I called home that evening from the apartment I shared with two friends not far from the stadium, then in its 56th year of existence. I don't remember what I said to Dad by way of expressing my horror, but I vividly remember what he said just before we finished our conversation.

"I won't live to see it, but you'll see a black president of the United States."

The whole notion was so unfathomably and uncharacteristically asinine that I didn't even respond. And yet my father turned out to be right on all counts: in 1966, the very next year, he'd drop dead, breaking my heart; and I would live to see Barack Obama serve two terms as America's chief executive.

If only that interlude could have changed my country as much as millions of us hoped.

I recall something else from my June afternoon in 1951, something very odd indeed, given all that transpired that day. Brief as my glimpse of the beaten man had been, as we rode home in silence, I remember thinking that his face, unwrinkled and youthfully handsome, resembled the face of Willie Mays. This was not a matter of racial identity, not one of those abhorrent they-all-look-alike surmises. The supine man on the pavement did not remind me at all, say, of Willie's African-American teammates Monte Irvin and Hank Thompson. It just somehow struck me that the downed man, given far different circumstances, might break into a dynamic smile, full, yes, of verve and elan.

That notion puzzled the hell out of me, and I badly wanted to purge it from my mind— which would take a lot longer than I might have predicted. In fact, to this day I obviously haven't succeeded.

A few days ago, I longed for something akin to the smile I longed for that day from the policemen's victim. And I felt a deep, seemingly disproportionate sorrow as I held the dead cardinal in my hand, perhaps hoping that the bird could be restored to its beautiful liveliness. I knew enough of the world now to see the vanity of such magical thinking, and so, though I hated to do it, I stepped inside, lifted the top of our woodstove, and dropped in that small, brilliant body, which felt almost as light as air.

Sydney Lea

KEEPAWAY
–for Stephen Bluestone

The day was autumn-gray, with a flock of migrant starlings squalling above the schoolyard din. Meddlesome blasts of wind kept tipping my oversized baseball cap. I heard the older boys' humbling laughter at my efforts to hold the hat on with one hand while stretching for the ball with the other.

I still picture the ball's every scuff and dent as it passed above, seeming to hang there, as if tethered to something unseen in that ashen sky. The faded blue of its rubber, a barely perceptible reddish ring around its girth– these remain clear to me even now. I simply couldn't grab that ball, but at least it represented a tangible goal, unlike the nameless one or ones I would later crave.

This all brings a not entirely rueful smile to my face: what if the ball had not escaped me, if by luck or cunning, I'd actually managed to grip it? Such longing, such paltry reward! But yes, I would have held it, known it.

The ungraspable, ever-nameless adult goals were likely paltry too. Whatever they may have been, I recognized one day that my hunger for them had evaporated. Or had it been satisfied long before and I'd suddenly and unconsciously awakened to that given?

Such Dancing as We Can

I look outdoors at the greening springtime field. There has always been so much available if I choose to see it, so much that I feel actual guilt at the sumptuousness all around me.

I consider that pair of mallards sculling on the pond, for one little instance. The drake's green head rebounds the sun, and the hen's blue primaries are a kindred if subtler marvel. I catch an oddly pleasant redolence of skunk cabbage, and through the trees, their leaves still small, I can make out splashes of gold from a sprawl of marsh marigolds.

A phoebe is making her nest by the garden. She loudly announces her name from the crown of a flowering crab.

Sydney Lea

UNHOLY

I'd awakened from a dream of a wedding. Wraith-like figures patrolled a stone church's aisles, which appeared to flow deep crimson. So, by the time I saw the blood on my grandmother's sheet, I'd already been seized by terror.

Before the snowstorm, our parents flew to some warm place we children had never heard of. They tried to soothe us by saying their trip was a second honeymoon. Tension, though no outright conflict, had prowled the house through the preceding six months or so. I suspected my five-year-old brother sensed it, and maybe even the three-year-old, too.

Our grandmother, when left to mind us, imposed little discipline. As a rule, I rejoiced when she baby-sat, although at seven, I disliked anyone's calling it that. This time, however, I did not celebrate.

Whatever their motive, our parents' departure felt like a monstrous threat. It struck me hardest in the early hours of the second night: they had plain abandoned their children. Not that their treatment of us was always exemplary, but I knew it to be as good as what many of my friends got, and a lot better than some did.

Such Dancing as We Can

We called our grandmother Nanny. That night, her bedroom window revealed a cluster of oak leaves below, fallen at last in late winter, lying still as corpses on the new snow. In the flagrant moonlight, the garden also teemed with other, weirder shapes. I knew these were merely shadow-blotches, laid down by clouds crossing the moon, but this knowledge failed to reassure me.

The blood on her blankets, I understood, must surely be nothing but shadows too– and still I was scared. I'd never known such quiet. In my mind, the silence and stillness portended something awful.

Though I couldn't predict what unholy rites would go into that grotesque wedding I'd conjured in my sleep, I knew they were going to be brutal. *You only dreamed it,* I kept telling myself, yet I stood spellbound at Nanny's door, a paralysis that seemed to go on and on. I feared the old woman's breathing might have stopped. Still, I balked at stirring her to find out, no matter how much I ached for adult comfort. If she were dead, that was horror enough. But if she came to – and I have no idea why I thought this way– the dream's malevolent agents might return.

Dream-bride and groom each wielded a weapon in one hand, some book – black magic scripture? – in the other. In fact, I couldn't precisely identify either weapon or book, but like all in the congregation, I understood both were deadly. The couple glared along the pews where we all sat wordless, afraid that the slightest sound or movement might provoke them to mayhem. Even after seven decades, I shudder to recall the cruelty in their eyes.

I had sat, Sunday after Sunday, in our easygoing Episcopal congregation with the frail little lady I watched now, while my parents were doing…who knew? Assuming she was indeed alive, that tiny woman would surely be of no help to my younger brothers and me, should the actions of the bride and groom turn dire.

At length, I found the courage to move from Nanny's doorway, but I slid my feet along the floor, avoiding the noise of actual steps. Back in bed, I leaned against the headboard, its panel chill on the skin of my neck, and waited – interminably, it seemed – for daylight.

Such Dancing as We Can

FORGIVENESS

My fourth grade teacher abused me at every turn, no matter I was a good kid –or maybe not that, but certainly not really a bad one.

Once, for example, the man accused me of writing some wise-guy story, when truth was, I meant only to compose a comic one. Sneering, he read it aloud to the class to demonstrate my unpardonable irreverence. I still hear his voice, deliberately turned mousey; I see his curled lip as he speaks. As I say, all I'd intended was comedy.

Believe me, I found no humor in what he called me the morning after my commonplace playground tussle with my good friend Monty, during which Monty fell and dislocated a vertebra in his neck. That meant he'd die, I knew, and I cried all night at the prospect of his death but equally of my own. Everyone understood that such a crime meant the electric chair. It was all so unjust: I'd meant no harm at all. You couldn't even have called it a fight. No one felt angry.

Thank God, Monty came to school next day, wearing a big Elizabethan collar. He also wore a grin –a bit self-conscious but genial– as if nothing unusual had happened. No matter: that sadistic schoolmaster called me "Man-Killer" in front of everyone, which reduced me to tears again. My reaction wasn't logical, because there my friend was, sitting at his regular desk. Yet the preceding night's emotions, especially after so little sleep, had lingered, barely under the surface.

By now, the tyrant who often beat me, who constantly humiliated me in front of my friends and, far worse, enemies like George Piglio and Billy Legrand, is doubtless long dead. No matter, I find myself looking for an old-fashioned curse. I'm sure none has ever really worked, but I'll give it a try anyhow.

Wherever he is, may my old teacher wear a collar like Monty's, but lined with biting insects, and may someone yank it up over his head, abrading his ears as he did mine when I tried on my new peewee football pads, excited right after they'd been issued in the gym. Let someone rip the collar off, thrust it on again, rip it off, on and off, the bugs feasting, forever and ever, amen. Let someone magically turn *him* into a child for a spell, then lay on all this punishment in reprimand for normal childish behavior.

But no: here I am, come to think, flinging invective back his way over sixty years and more, even though he's surely long dead, and I, still alive, having purged such spleen at last, should be able to pray, as I do, that he rest in peace– the bastard.

Such Dancing as We Can

LIKE GRANT TOOK RICHMOND

By the time I got old enough to understand as much, I recognized that my grandmother's genteel sayings had eclipsed the Germanic ones of her childhood. For example, *Great Caesar's Ghost!* replaced *gooka mol!* if my grandmother wanted to call attention to something spectacular: a cloud, maybe, in the shape of Billy Penn's hat atop Philadelphia's city hall, a particularly colorful bird, what have you. Still, as I stood behind her on the sofa-sized backseat of her Packard one day, we passed another car, on fire at roadside. *Ferschrecka!* she barked. Such an incident would repeat itself now and then, however infrequently.

That grandmother was Pennsylvania Dutch. Just before her birth, her parents had moved the family from the countryside closer to town, and their vernacular must gradually have faded with the geographical change. Or, as likely, they quashed it in order to accommodate a less provincial neighborhood.

We all lived with her in the rambling house where she'd been born and where she'd borne our mother. I was the eldest child of an eventual five.

Though it didn't occur to me to think about it as a boy, in retrospect I'm stunned that my grandmother's own birth in 1878 should have come a mere thirteen years after the Emancipation Proclamation and Lee's capitulation at Appomattox.

A generation always believes it's the one to have experienced revolution, but think of everything my grandmother saw between her arrival on earth and her departure almost a century later: the transition from horse-drawn carriage to automobile; women's exercise of the right to vote; Prohibition and its repeal. She lost a son to the 1918 influenza pandemic; she knew the deep malaise and tragedy of two world wars. On and on. She watched humans walk on the moon– *what in tarnation?*– and she died as the cybernetic era dawned.

For all the precipitous change in her world, however, she did now and then fetch up those old-time expressions, or rather, in certain circumstances they erupted from her. Afterwards, her countenance always turned uneasy.

I haven't any idea why I should recall her quaint expressions in both idioms when justified black anger kindles all over the country. You'd think that some things I heard from our father would come to mind instead. As I mentioned early on, Dad commanded a company of so-called colored troops in World War II.

Such Dancing as We Can

After the war, there'd be no GI bill provided for those troops, no subsidies for their farms, no bank loans, no scholarships for their children. It's high time for reparations, though I'm not sure what shape they might take. I don't pretend to be a great thinker, but yes, I can recognize obscenity.

For murky reasons, I've lately been thinking too of how we brothers could rage, even closing our fists now and then. This strife went on during another war, the half-forgotten one in Korea. *You're a caution to snakes!* Grandmother might shout if we turned particularly rowdy, or *You've run through this place like Grant took Richmond!* But we were just little kids; no one really got hurt.

In later life, we two boys– a third long dead– and two sisters sustain loving relationships, no matter we're scattered all over the east. And we stay bonded primarily by way of invisible electrons. Think of it: how things have changed!

But some still haven't. So much just hasn't.

Sydney Lea

Orange Order Fair, 1951

I had no idea why the old stranger sitting right under the stage would call me to his side. It turned out he just wanted me to admire his shirt, which was made of some shiny orange cloth with little spangles of silver scattered over it.

"Fancy!" I said.

Pleased enough by that, he started chattering about his life. I felt indifferent to his reminiscences, but I kept nodding politely. I did face slightly away from him because his breath smelled strange, nasty.

The 13th of July meant nothing to me, except that it seemed to occasion a fair in a field near my favorite boyhood haunt, my bachelor uncle's farm. Under a circus-like tent, a band played for some time after we arrived. The music sounded like nothing I'd ever heard, but you could tell the crowd liked it.

The uncle's hired man, my best friend Eddie's father, had brought us. He frightened me some. He was of below-average height, but his bulging, sun-bronzed arms seemed things that *ought* to frighten a boy, or anyone, really. He came from County Louth, wherever that was.

Such Dancing as We Can

Eddie and I wandered for a while through barns full of cattle, pigs, sheep and draft horses, or duller stuff like quilts, jams, pies and giant squashes, until his father found us and led us to a table under the tent. The punch in the kids' bowls was a different color from the grownups'. Theirs looked smoky; ours was orange. For some reason, Eddie's mom drank from the orange one. Everybody loved her, but to me she always looked a little sad.

I had trouble understanding most of the visitors to our table, who talked like Eddie's dad. The food was plain old hot dogs and burgers, and they weren't that good, really.

After lunch, some men climbed onto the stage, including the old fellow who'd showed off his shirt. Another man, not quite as old, put a medal of some kind around the neck of the one with the shirt, who stroked it as if it were a teddy bear or something. He waved to the crowd and started to sniffle. I felt a little embarrassed to see a grownup crying like that.

Unlike him, all the others talked. And talked. Each one mentioned the Battle of the Boyne, whenever that was, and wherever. I thought it might be Korea, which the grownups at my house kept talking about. That, and a man named McCarthy, who was not a good person, they thought, though there were several pictures of him at various spots on the fairgrounds.

Sydney Lea

After everyone ate, the speeches started up again. I glanced at Eddie, and I could read his mind; I mean, we were *really* close friends. We made to get up from our chairs, but his father sat him back down, holding him there by one shoulder of the dress-up shirt he'd worn to church that morning. I sat down again too.

All I had on were jeans, a T-shirt, and a pair of Keds, so my attire wasn't up to the occasion, I guess, but by then I'd stopped worrying about the look of my clothes. I only wanted to jump out of them and into the pool Eddie and I had made the day before. We'd pushed rocks around all afternoon to dam a stream on my uncle's back property. It was hard work.

Suddenly, one of the people onstage shouted, "The battle continues!" A huge roar filled the tent. It made me jump. When the noise finally died down, the same speaker made a very loud toast to people he called *loyal friends.* Like everything else, the toast went on forever. The list of names he read must have been long as his leg. The whole business seemed pretty boring to me, but when he finished, the crowd cheered and stomped even more wildly. That scared me all over again.

The last man onstage wobbled over to the microphone just after the applause and shouting died down. He started yelling as well, except when he used certain phrases, which he hissed. The only one I recall was "The Scarlet Whore of Babylon" He whispered that several times, and whenever he did, people hissed too, or just booed.

What he meant by *whore* I couldn't really be sure back then, but somehow I knew it was a word you needed to whisper, something no woman would ever say– not that there were any women on that platform.

The old man in tears, his shirt, the enormous beasts in the barns, the two kinds of punch, the loudness of the crowd– for me, that day's mostly snatches of memory. Were the speeches clever? I wasn't sure one way or another. People did seem to like them.

At about three, we headed home, Eddie's mom at the wheel, which was very unusual. His dad napped all the way there. In the backseat, we did our own whispering. We swore we'd be friends forever.

And we stayed true to that pledge right along– until I left for college and Eddie stayed on the farm.

Sydney Lea

A Neighbor's Daydream

On one of our countless visits, the neighbor showed me how she sat in the kitchen as a young girl —elbows propped on the table's tacky oilcloth, chin in hands— and look out the window, gloomy.

Angry too. She didn't know why in those days. She forgot much of her rage whenever she escaped to the library in the village. Although I was just a kid, I could tell that she she'd read a lot of books in her time.

I can't remember exactly when I started to drop in at that moldering, drafty house, all the woman had left of her farm, which bordered my uncle's. To a boy with a complicated home life, the uncle's place made a haven. So did hers.

Once, I whined that my parents meant to ship me off to college someday, and I didn't want to go. Her expression darkened for a moment, then she sighed. I understand today.

With her husband long dead, her three sons moved far away, she was all alone. That's probably what made me so welcome in her last five years or so, which consisted mostly of reminiscence. I didn't mind. For whatever reason, her stories always gripped me, even something plain, like how her father built a bench for himself by the dooryard elm and sat there when weather was fine.

His idea was to keep the stench of his evening cigar out of the house, especially after his wife started wheezing, a trouble that worsened with time. That kind of thoughtfulness, my neighbor assured me, showed the man's simple decency. She recollected this in such vivid detail— which hat her father wore depending on the season, the way he crossed one leg at right angles to the other or closed his eyes with each puff of smoke, and so on— that I all but saw him on that rough seat.

As her health became direr and direr, her mother's cough grew more and more violent, and, apart from those worrisome sounds, the house got quieter and quieter. In desperation, the girl would frequently ask her parents if a cure might be found for the mysterious ailment. Neither ever chose to answer directly.

"They just looked helpless every time," the neighbor said. "That really disappointed me."

Her habit when she went to the library was simply to walk along a shelf, skimming her fingertips along the backs of books. Then, without looking, she'd stop on one, and she'd read as much of it as she could before the library closed. She admitted she stayed away from the science section, favoring history above all.

I remember her mentioning how she stopped once at a book about France in the Middle Ages, and how one part of it stuck in her craw for weeks: she recognized that her family would have been labeled *peasants* in those days, and in fact they'd still be called so in some places.

By serendipity, the next book she landed on when she finally went back to the library contained a section on peasants too, but it turned out that the *Ottoman* peasantry could get rowdy if anyone, no matter who, treated them condescendingly or imposed on them in any way at all. Sometimes they even resorted to violence, and sometimes the violence was organized. She spoke of this with something of a far-off look on her face.

"Those folks would've probably run off this man from the county who showed up one spring," the widow told me. "He cursed Dad out for quite a while about being late with our taxes."

Her color rose when she described the scene; it had clearly shamed her that her father just stood there and listened. Though she was stooped and small and wore the shapeless, floral-patterned sort of dress that housewives all seemed to wear back in the 40s and 50s, I could easily picture her getting ready for battle. An amazon, I'd have called her, if I'd known the word. Her fierce expression would have scared me if she hadn't been so friendly all those summers.

As it turned out, her mother would die rather quickly, and after she passed on my neighbor would tend to her father until his death, which came a considerable number of years later. So much for any aspirations beyond marriage when she finished high school.

If she got worked up about the county tax collector, she became even more so when she spoke of a certain fantasy that often came to her, especially under certain conditions.

"I'd have that daydream when it turned dusky out and the bats started flitting around the way they do," she said. "But it really got strong when a thunderstorm blew in." She described lightning carving up the sky, a warning that her vision was about to arrive.

That vision would slowly dissipate after her mother's death and evaporate entirely after her father's. While it prevailed, though, its setting and circumstances never varied. "This daydream was a whole lot different from what we lived," she said.

Sydney Lea

She'd be standing next to a marble fountain on a big sweep of lawn. She swore she heard the water's sound as it fell into the pool. From her position, she could look out and see horsemen, just silhouettes on the skyline at first. She fought to wake up so they'd disappear, but it didn't matter. They kept wildly racing right at her, and somehow she knew they meant to murder her mother and father.

"It's very strange," she told me, slowly shaking her head. "For just a second or two, that killing seemed as though it might be all right."

She always scrambled to add that the strange feeling died right off, and that it always horrified her to think she had had it in the first place.

"Oh yes, it stopped quick,", she stressed. "Yes, thank the Lord it stopped!"

Such Dancing as We Can

FAMILIAR STRANGER

He stepped into our general store, trailing a faintly smoky odor. I could just hear him humming a song, and though I didn't know why, something about it intrigued me, its cadences stirring a memory, for the moment ungraspable

The stranger's features were mostly as undistinctive as his clothing. Yet when he turned, his eyes had a ghostly quality, and when they locked on mine I swore I felt something like a burn. Had he singled me out from among our little knot of customers, and if so, why? I quickly looked away.

After a moment, undetected, I hoped, I turned back to watch him browse the shelves. He didn't seem to be after anything specific, but at length he chose a lighter. An incurable grasper after metaphor, if that's the right term here, I thought the choice accorded with the mild feverishness his presence had kindled in me. Yet I soon discovered I couldn't liken anything about him— tune, eyes, odor, or warmth— to anything or anyone else I could summon, figuratively or otherwise.

So what about him primed me to imagine misfortune?

Everyone in the store flinched when a siren erupted outside. That's a common enough sound in big cities, but we rarely hear it in our small upcountry village. Through the plate glass window, we all followed a state police cruiser as it shot by. All, that is, but the out-of-towner, who waited at the register with his back to us.

I didn't ask anyone else, but to me that shrill noise seemed more than just abnormal. It not only pierced the more or less pleasant routine of our neighborhood, but also, I thought, sent a cryptic signal from some unknown dominion. Pure nonsense, of course, as I well knew. Even so, it left me unsettled, to use an easy euphemism.

At last, the visitor nodded affably at our little group, shoved open the screen, and left, still humming that barely audible air.

My neighbors seemed scarcely to notice. They went on with their palaver, none beside me appearing the least concerned with this man but rather, quite understandably, with what that siren might signify.

Then I had it.

One autumn morning when I was thirteen, Eddie and I rode in the truck as his father hauled a boar hog to the abattoir. When we arrived, he told us not to get out, which we didn't dream of doing. My friend's dad was a man you took orders from.

Such Dancing as We Can

I heard the tailgate clank behind us. Turning to look out the rear window, I could tell the pig sensed something grim in the offing. An attendant, who smoked a short black cigar, prodded the poor thing into a chain-link passageway and then through a low steel door, which he emphatically slammed.

The man walked Eddie's dad back to the truck, and, for a minute or so, they conversed through its open window. Then, having stubbed his stogey, the attendant retreated into the squat, gray building by another entrance. Before the hired man cranked up the window, however, I clearly heard the other man whistle, though it was more like breathing. It was the tune I'd half-recognize more than sixty years later. I had caught a whiff of the abattoir worker's tobacco, but I chiefly noted his spectral eyes.

Just then I flinched at the sudden scream of a siren. Why did I never ask Eddie how any of this affected him?

The siren had only blown to announce the noon hour, but just after it wound down, a different scream poured out of the slaughterhouse. We boys squirmed when we heard it, and Eddie's father, so rugged and seasoned, sat staring through the windshield for what seemed a long, long moment, hands clenched on the steering wheel.

Sydney Lea

He started the engine, but its rumble came too late to cover that cry, which, these many decades later, I likewise failed to repress.

TOUGH LUCK

To me, like many, it seems an age since I started to read about hapless refugees persistently and frantically trying to poke holes through barriers at our southern border. How many have been shot down by now, I wonder? More than "reasons of state" will allow us to know, I suspect.

I leave justification for such abuse to our vile former president and his self-styled "Christian" advocates, though I can't help wondering if they're as versed in the Gospel as they claim to be. (It's perfectly clear Trump knows flat nothing of Scripture.) If indeed they are steeped in the Bible, what do you suppose they make of their Lord's words in Matthew? *I was hungry and you gave me food, I was thirsty and you gave me drink, I was a stranger and you welcomed me.* Or, since they seem more inclined to favor the punitive God of the Hebrew Bible, how do they deal with something like this from Leviticus? *You shall treat the stranger who sojourns with you as the native among you, and you shall love him as yourself, for you were strangers in the land of Egypt.*

As for me and Eddie, 65 or so years back, we would simply have ascribed the strangers' deaths and suffering to tough luck. We knew little about the conflicted world, and all we did know about ill fortune was paltry: flat tires on our bikes, birthday parties missed because of sickness, weekend games of pickup baseball squelched by rain, death of a pet, and so on.

Eddie and I used to shoot down the rats that gathered high in the cow barn's ivy when the sun dropped off. One of us shone the light, the other fired. Not that for one nanosecond I liken those desperate asylum-seekers to rodents. Soon enough, I'd come to learn more about poverty, oppression, violence –political or criminal or both– and to recognize that we boys were a thousand times blessed compared to a numberless population of the truly wretched.

It *was* only tough luck that made one nasty moment for Eddie. The incident could well have come my way, but this time I happened to be the one with the gun while he focused the beam at a crackle in the foliage above.

Both of us were partly motivated by smug and ignorant righteousness: rats killed chicks, sucked eggs, and so on. It's not that I came to love rats in my maturity but that looking back, I marvel at the joy we took in slaughter, not only of them but also, say, of crows, which we misjudged as enemies of the farm. They cleaned up carrion, and they killed rats too, a fact we ignored if we were ever aware of it. We'd been told by adults that crows were guilty of stealing seed corn, pulling shoots from the vegetable

Such Dancing as We Can

garden, and assorted other offenses. The crows were far too smart for us to make much of a dent in their numbers; if, though, we did manage to bag one or two, how satisfying to be told that our bloodthirstiness was a service to my uncle's property.

But back to Eddie's misadventure. I managed to shoot one big rat, which clung momentarily to the ivy, fell from wall to ground– and scooted up inside one of his pantlegs! Before the poor animal dropped out, which must have seemed an hour to my buddy, I could see by moonlight that his eyes were a welter of fears, that his face had turned ghastly.

And there I stood, wanting to help, but what could I do?

As for that, what *can* I?

Why connect today's brutal headlines about events on the banks of the Rio Grande to that night when Eddie aimed the light and I killed a frantic rat? Yes, the wounded animal scrabbled for shelter and so you could accurately call it a refugee; but any effort to forge a whole here, to connect our slaughter with the horrors facing human refugees, is laborious and, worse, fatuous.

It's just that I'm still attracted, I guess, even as I recognize its simplism and ultimate inanity, to a less complicated view of the world, one in which my moral muscles might relax. Eddie and I made no efforts at analogizing the local and the general, not back when things appeared to be so easy, when justice looked so clear to two barely adolescent boys, when a victim's anguish was a matter we never considered. If calamity struck someone, as when the rat shinnied up my buddy's calf, it was only a random thing.

Tough luck.

Such Dancing as We Can

UNKNOWN SAINTS

As for most, my early adolescence was an uneasy time. Mixed parties began to happen, with games of Post Office, Spin-the-Bottle, and others— much needed, since initiating any interaction with the opposite sex seemed hopeless, at least to me. I just couldn't seem to kick my shyness.

Was I the one, or was it Bruce, or perhaps my nemesis Phil, who contrived the notion of forming a band? We needed some ploy to blunt our loneliness, though in fact, I have no business saying *we*, because I wished small luck on Bruce and still less on Phil.[1]

Those unreachable girls would politely lift needles from their Elvis tunes and endure our efforts. Phil sat at some household's piano, Bruce blew his trumpet, and I played clarinet.

We had a paltry repertoire, just two or three half-learned numbers to labor through before we offered our self-styled, and consistently unsolicited encore, *When the Saints Go Marching In,* which was as close to rock n roll as folks had discovered by then. White folks, that is: we didn't know R&B, any more than we did that our signature song derived from Second Line, up-tempo numbers performed as funeral processions returned from New Orleans's so-called colored graveyards over half a century before.

These unnamed saints coaxed jitterbug wiggles out of us witless young Caucasians,

Here and throughout I have changed many of my "characters'" names.

gathered in living rooms with rugs rolled up to walls. Did I dream of a wife or children,

let alone grandchildren, back then? That seems unlikely, but even if I did, I doubt I imagined they'd one day be my heart's desire.

Today is such a day, though for the moment I am quite alone. The late-May sounds of upper New England seem to add a further touch of shame to the shameful old sounds I recollect. Tree frogs trill their melodies and water coursing in freshets is undersong to other wondrous music around me.

Meanwhile I'm stunned at how more than fifty years have gone by while I've lived here beside rough dirt roads in stamp-sized towns in far northern states. Scarcely for the first time, I marvel at fate: there are so many different other ways in which I might have fashioned a life. By this

Such Dancing as We Can

time, however, I just can't imagine them. I'm old enough too that I wouldn't really want to.

Though this world appears so distinct from that old one I conjure, I can hear Bruce's trumpet in the black flies' hum; Phil misses the third in a chord– it's a raven; a blue jay squawks from the crown of a hemlock– my reed's got a chip. For the briefest instant, I'm again as guileless and baffled by the world as I was back then, when a makeshift, discordant trio strove to invite those unknown saints into our lives.

Sydney Lea

FANTASIES IN '56

Hank Nicci worked as the pump attendant at Greville's Sunoco all that summer. He had a softball-sized Valentine heart tattooed on one shoulder. It read *Mom*– what else in those days, unless you were a Navy man?

Hank's girlfriend was the prettiest woman I'd ever seen. She drove a smoking-hot '48 Mercury with some newer and bigger V-8 under the hood. Its glass-pack mufflers made a guttural rumble as it idled, but a roar– louder, more thrilling– when she tromped the throttle. That scarlet Merc glistened like a candy apple. What I wouldn't have done for a street rod like that!

Her family must have had money. The car was much customized, and was so radically lowered that sparks sprayed from its bumpers whenever she drove onto the lot. Just watching her arrive made my own sparks fly, which of course she never imagined. Her name was Roy-Anne, and I knew if I were ever to tell my mother about her, she'd announce that my dream-love was cheap.

Roy-Anne and Hank could fight like wildcats. I once heard her scream, "You can kiss my ass!" before peeling out of the station. How could that have thrilled me so too? If such cursing or anything else about her meant she was cheap, well, cheap was all I longed for. Bad language.

Cool automobile. Hell, I'd kiss her wherever and as much as she pleased. On the rare occasions when she got out of her Mercury, I'd invent some way to get close to her, and I got dizzy just whiffing her scent– perfume, shampoo and spearmint gum.

What kind of idiot could Hank be? He didn't seem to think about Roy-Anne's feelings at all. She could scream her lungs out at him, and he still wouldn't lay off flirting with every woman who drove in. Why did he risk losing her? I kept thinking I'd behave however she told me to if Roy-Anne were my sweetheart.

Just say the word, I whispered one evening. She didn't hear, needless to say.

I was old enough for summer work, but still too young to drive, so after mucking out stalls or pitching hay or driving turkeys at my uncle's place, I had to thumb my way down to Greville's, where I hung out every late afternoon until suppertime. My hope that one day Roy-Anne would be driving by and would stop to give me a ride didn't come true. None of my hopes did.

Truth is, in those days I'd have hung out at the Sunoco, pretty girl or no. For one thing and for whatever reason, Hank seemed to enjoy having me around. I loved sizing up the various cars that came in with him, sneering at the four-door family sedans and station wagons, lusting for the V-8 coupes. All this enthralled me, no matter how many lectures I got from my mom about wasting precious hours at *a dirty old gas station.* I never told her anything, naturally, about Roy-Anne, or much of anything else.

Mom pressured me to set my sights as high as I could, often using the phrase "bright years ahead." I needed to work hard, she insisted, so that I could be admitted to what she called a good college. Otherwise, there wouldn't *be* any bright years. Once I got to an Ivy League campus, she claimed, I'd discover new goals. As for me, since I'd never found any goals in school, I wondered why on earth I'd discover them in college.

My only goal that summer was to turn into Hank Nicci– big arms, red tattoo, giggly housewives blushing and spluttering as I filled their gas tanks, and above all a girlfriend like Roy-Anne. I don't know how many times I heard her shout and curse, but she stayed with Hank at least until I did go off to a famous university.

What I truly believed back then seems laughable now, though not quite entirely: if I couldn't find someone exactly like Roy-Anne, I figured I'd just up and die.

Well, I've lived a long, long time without her, thank heavens, or anyone like her, and long ago I found a

Such Dancing as We Can

woman every bit as beautiful, not just on the outside— in her soul as well. But when I was fourteen, yes, I plain ached for that girl! It was so frustrating, because, unlike Hank, I'd have treated her well enough that she might even have let me, at least now and then, switch spots on the seat and take the Merc's wheel.

Sydney Lea

1957

The whole thing mystified me at age fifteen. It hasn't puzzled me for a long time. I'm less troubled by it too, even if the event does still leave me oddly uneasy.

One Saturday, I was walking back from the school ball field. We hadn't gotten enough boys together for a game, so we just played catch, shagged flies, and so on. Mostly, we told our exaggerated stories, though no one believed anyone else's. That's why for years I shared this experience with a single school friend. Too many would have thought I was fibbing.

Within a quarter-mile of home, I heard music blaring from a radio. Who wouldn't have wanted to find out what that commotion amounted to? I followed it to the Ds' house, a place very familiar to me. I crossed the front lawn when I didn't see Mr. D's car in the drive. He was a bit daunting, with his Navy tattoos, an anchor on one arm and a mermaid on the other, not to mention his drinking like… well, like a sailor, often right from the bottle, as if his whiskey were Coke or something. After he'd had a few pulls, he'd start making light-hearted wisecracks, but he could turn grumpy and worse without any warning whatsoever. I never risked knocking on the Ds' door unless their daughter Dolly was home, and even then I got nervous until I could be sure her father had his mood more or less under control.

Dolly and I were steadies, but she was away at a camp in Maine where she'd been going for years and years. I sometimes wondered why she hadn't gotten tired of the place. In any case, since she was an only child, I knew her mother must be alone.

Her daughter called Mrs. D a *bottle-blonde*. She smirked a little when she said that, but only because she was envious. Dolly was nice-looking, all right– just not in her mom's league.

The Ds' lived close to us, and I knew the house well. My own parents disapproved of television, so we didn't have one at home. In fact, the Ds' TV set may have accounted as much as anything for my interest in their daughter. You don't have to tell me that sounds terrible. Looking back, I need no help in beating myself up about it– and plenty else.

I remember dark winter afternoons after school, when we two would go down to the basement and tune in "Queen for a Day," which we liked to poke fun at. Some poor old lady would weep with joy over the washing machine or the oven or the medical help she was going to get just for being the most miserable person to have reported her woes to the studio by mail. The sadder the tale, the louder the applause. As I look back, that seems an odd sort of win, but we didn't think about such a matter.

Dolly and I also engaged, when we dared, in some teenage groping. Nothing too heavy, though.

One day as we watched our program, just holding hands, she and I felt as though *we* were the ones being watched. It turned out that Bobo, a squat neighborhood mongrel, part Dalmatian, part basset, was out there in the fog, his sorry face peering through the window. From then on, we noticed how he showed up whenever we had the set on.

"He must look at *TV Guide*," Dolly joked after the third or fourth time.

I've strayed from my story, which back then I never dreamed was almost as dismal as the ones on "Queen for a Day." I'll go back to it now, but please understand that, even as an adolescent, when hormones made me half-crazy at times, I was never some creepy voyeur. It wouldn't be right to blame me for what happened.

The ear-splitting music was something slow and corny, all trembly strings. When I looked through Bobo's window, I saw Dolly's mom holding her mop handle like a microphone stand in the TV room. She was obviously singing, although I couldn't hear her over the radio. Her eyes were half-closed, and all she had on was frilly black underwear, the kind I'd seen once when an older cousin showed me his *Playboys*. They were worlds different from the silken bloomers my mother hung on the clothesline.

I wanted to run, but before I could, Mrs. D opened her eyes and stared right at me. It was as though she knew I'd be there. I froze, nowhere to go. To my astonishment, she smiled in a strange, woozy way and waved me around to her cellar door. I felt I had to obey, even though I desperately wanted to escape.

After she opened up, Mrs. D reeled back to that basement room. I dutifully followed, trying not to watch her jiggle. Suddenly, she swiveled and hugged me, all in one motion. At first I froze again, almost fainting with shyness, no matter that, like every boy in my circle, I always said I'd give my right arm for a moment more or less like this one. She really was pretty as a movie star.

I kept my head turned away, so she didn't embrace me for more than a few seconds. Letting out a big sigh, or rather a huff, she grabbed a blue robe from a chair, put it on, and led me— no, pushed me— back to where I'd come in.

What had I done to make her so angry?

Next day, swearing him to secrecy, I told my classmate Patrick about the event, though I didn't really go into detail. Once he saw I wasn't lying, Pat said I had to repent, a word I wasn't used to hearing. I didn't know many Catholics apart from his family. His dad worked for the Knights of Columbus, though I'm not sure what his job was. In any case, I couldn't see how I'd go about repenting, or even quite why, and my friend didn't go into it any further.

Truth is, I believe he was jealous. He kept pressing me for more than I wanted to give. I told him that she wore those lacey underthings and that she hugged me, but everything else I left vague. Of course, there wasn't much else, come to think of it.

Well, there *was* one thing. In that briefest of moments, I could feel Mrs. D's heart and mine beating together. I remember the sensation quite well, maybe better than anything else from that afternoon.

After she shoved me outdoors, I stood in my tracks for a minute or two. Then I walked over and looked through the little window again. She'd turned off her radio and stood the mop in its bucket. Still wearing the robe, she stood there herself, not even moving, except for her hands, which she kept clenching and unclenching. She was crying.

Such Dancing as We Can

Strange: I suddenly felt that I cared more about Dolly than I ever had before. And yet I couldn't imagine how I'd face her when she got back from camp, let alone how I'd face her mom. I'd have to write Dolly a letter if I could find her address up there. I'd just say we were through; there didn't seem any way to tell her why. I just couldn't go down to that basement again. The whole business made me pretty unhappy.

I knew this meant no more TV, but that was a long way from what bothered me most– not that I can precisely identify what the real trouble was even now.

I don't know how old Mrs. D was when she died, which was not that long after, in my college years. She was at least a good deal younger than my own mom, who, when I asked her about Mrs. D's death, simply told me, with a slight sneer on her face, *She always liked her wine.*

Sydney Lea

Mrs. Ragnetti and the Spider

Still warm this morning, autumn's chill yet to come. An angler spider, trailing its thread, precisely, like a fishing line, has just caught me, in perfect coincidence with my random recall of *la signora Ragnetti*. In memory, the woman remains the ogre who terrified me every Thursday afternoon all through a winter. At singing lessons, fist on high, she led me, barely turned tenor, through cheerless versions of *Caro mio ben'* and others. My mother had sent me to her. I've tasted hell. It is with me now in present tense.

I arrive, cradling my folio of airs, sopped and stained by the smutty snow of this stranger's land, the asphalt city. The bells of San Cristofero's drone a torpid portent of the agony ahead. It seems I hear the teacher even before I knock on the door: "How is this? You do not do these things I tell you, so simple. *O Dio, che stupido....*"

The spider must think he's found arachnid heaven: that is, if a spider may be said to think. He surely considers me quite a catch, not knowing how I've shrunk. He's likely drunk with joy, unaware of how in those old sessions, when (*cretino! farnullone!*) failure seemed its own long season, I was hollowed out to a specter. If the spider tweaked his thread, I'd rise. I'm only air in this nightmare, a whiff of ether.

Such Dancing as We Can

How can Mrs. Ragnetti, at five feet and perhaps ninety pounds, appear so huge? She wrests the door and impatiently waves me in, clicking her tongue. "So different from my son," she growls, before I've even removed my spattered jacket. She turns to study the son's photograph on a table. A middle-aged man stares out, face set and stern as her own. She crosses herself, scowls, then sits malignly down. Soon, too soon, her left hand jabs at scales on her piano, the right one clamped in that gnarled fist, as if she held a dagger.

"Piu forte!" she insists. I flinch, as though from actual blows, while we *do-re-mi*.

"*Desastro!*" she spits while I grapple up and down those ladders, no matter I know my voice, however timid, finds the pitch of each note exactly: "Do you come to me for making a noise?" Another note, another Latin imprecation. I grow colder, colder– and smaller. Once I've returned home, I know my mother will reject any complaints as self-pitying, puling, craven. She's been assured that *la signora* is the region's premiere voice coach. Am I not up to excellence?

Released at last, I cross the street to buy an icy milkshake, laced with malt, scant consolation for all I've felt go out of me. It's an effort directly counter to reason: the treat, rather than numbing me, seems to freeze even harder the

fear I'd meant to melt, the poisonous residue of terror,
hate.

Once I felt the ruthlessness of la Ragnetti. Now a spider
imagines it'll lift me into its maw.

Such Dancing as We Can

MENTOR

The only thing people really knew about him– apart from the fact even during that scalding hot summer, he always wore something with long sleeves– was that he'd leased the Wymans' old trailer. Mrs. Wyman figured he had nightmares. She'd often hear him screaming after dark; but he didn't cause any trouble otherwise, she said, and he always paid his rent right on time.

Our gang liked the library, which is where we met him. He was surprisingly pleased that we wanted to spend time there, even though in all honesty for us it was mostly a hangout on weekends, when we weren't at summer jobs. The librarian was a sweetheart; she didn't seem to mind our chatter if we weren't disturbing other visitors.

The stranger claimed to be doing research for a novel. Once or twice he gave us a rapid-fire summary of how the book would go. When he said that it had partly to do with heroin, we thought he must mean *heroine*. When he cursed the drug, we figured his female protagonist was an evil one indeed. In short, we were confused, but were too sheepish to ask for clarification. In time, we came to understand that he meant it concerned an addict, a term we barely knew. His book would chronicle his character's constant, reckless, and finally fatal behavior.

Sydney Lea

The man often fell asleep at a little table in a dark corner of the reading room, but awake, he was eager to talk. I recall his stained seersucker jacket, his command of big words, his yellowed moustache, but more than anything else his expression, always so tired. No wonder he slept, though what caused the fatigue was a mystery.

Miss Tyler, our librarian, treated that summer's stranger well, but then she treated everybody well. She reminded us of Cinderella's fairy godmother in the Disney film. She may well have known more than we did about this fellow, but she never said a word.

Our friend Walt was clearly Miss Tyler's pet, though his only difference from us was how well he could draw, which he did more than he read. When he did take down a book, it was always one about artists he claimed were famous, with reproductions of their work. He showed me a drawing one day by someone named Schiele, asking if it didn't depict agony in an extraordinary way. I agreed. I wanted to go along with Walt, though the sketch struck me as ugly.

Walt noticed things. For example, he was the first of us to mention how often the stranger scratched and rubbed at himself, especially at his neck. When he did, we saw marks like bug bites on every knuckle and in between and on both his wrists.

Such Dancing as We Can

Who cared? He cared about *us* and we were glad we'd met him.

Every time he spoke of the woman in his novel, his eyes got wet, which intrigued us, although it also put us a little on edge. We didn't really know how to respond to that display, but he didn't seem to demand a response; he'd quickly start talking again.

"Oh, the gifts she had!" he'd sigh. "Why on earth would she waste them?" It was just as if he were describing a real person, someone he actually knew.

Just before he vanished, he advised us to do something useful with our lives.

We all did, to one degree or another– except for poor Walt, who, after half year at art school in Rhode Island, died drugged and alone one Philadelphia winter, having dropped out of art school in Rhode Island. We'd all lost touch with him, but still we were sad when we heard.

What a waste, we thought. He was so gifted.

Sydney Lea

BATTLE OF THE HORNS

I haven't played the instrument for many, many years, but in the periodic and enduring effort to clean out closets, I came upon it, still gorgeous, shiny and black in its maroon velvet case. Could I still manage a tune or two? I decided not even to try, lulled instead into bitter reverie.

Cats and dogs? I inwardly scoffed. They don't know how to fight. My brother and I could have taught them a thing or two– no, a whole lot more than that!

I played that clarinet and my brother played French horn. Horn players, it seems, lead shorter lives, which I didn't learn until quite a while later. Like everything else, our instruments were tools of war. His big bell would bray at me, and my slender one screech back at him. What a racket! And what fools we were, our only on earth not to harmonize, not at all. We literally fought to shatter harmony.

Sometimes the family's actual cats and dogs would howl in alarm. And I remember a day when a squirrel outside froze on its limb for an instant, then hauled ass as high up the sick window-elm as possible.

A brain hemorrhage killed my brother at 35.

Such Dancing as We Can

In contemplating and regretting life's copious mistakes,
I've often wondered, what was all that wrangling *for?*
Wasn't there at least some touch of love underneath it all?
Forty years after his death, I try to recall traces of better
feelings, and better sounds than those squalls we made,
louder even than the hail that just now slams the metal
roof over me, as if to burst the ceiling.

Sydney Lea

WITHOUT GRACE

> Now you will not swell the rout
> Of lads that wore their honours out…
>   –A.E. Housman

Once shaped like the smirky smile of a cynic, that scar on my calf—a bit above my slightly arthritic left ankle– has somehow turned downward. It vaguely resembles the well-remembered frown of our hockey coach, who frequently reprimanded me for some graceless, feckless play I'd made.

There are notions that, even as an old man, I apparently can't relinquish. Deep inside, I still yearn to be Bob Feller, Y.A. Tittle, and above all Gordie Howe, or any childhood hero, really, who never appeared to doubt himself.

If only pompon-wielding girls had mounted a cheer for me alone! One of them might have wanted my ring. Or someone, *anyone,* my autograph. Sometime.

Might have.

The sky overhead is still the sky. It's still devoid of signature or sign. And I remain what I am and was, and nothing more.

Yes, much has turned to pallor, but some pains abide, undeniably *there*. Most are dull by now, true enough, but some still aren't. I recall especially that bull-shouldered defenseman's stick, which, like the vaudeville hook, yanked me by the neck and off my skates. The thug got ejected; I got a nasty gash just below the occipital bone on my right side. That scar is buried under hair, which, unlike its vanished kin on top, endures there.

Coach, inspecting blood on my jersey, seemed oddly satisfied, and oddly reluctant to see me driven to the clinic.

And oh, that impossibly beauteous nurse in her crisp white uniform!

My speech hindered by longing and by rushing ether, I watched the mask swell with my whisper: *"so graceful…"*

She appeared to consider the delicate gold watch on her unblemished wrist.

I must be wrong to recall a yawn.

Sydney Lea

SIXTY STEPS FROM YALE

"Maybe I'll try that special," my new friend Joe said with a derisory smile. The six of us had lingered outside just long enough to note the sign in the diner's window touting The Baseball Special, which consisted of a hotdog and two hard-boiled eggs. Needless to say, mere college freshmen that we were, we swapped mindless humor about what may well have been the owner's own intentional, ribald humor.

None of us yet knew that owner's name, because this wee-hour foray to the United came during our first all-nighter, that timeless freshman rite. Sam insisted he'd pulled one in high school, though the rest of us, innocent of any such experience, were loudly skeptical. Our little group shared a patent if unspoken exhilaration at the prospect of hitting the books, however casually, until the sun came up, shedding the confinements of household rules and curfews.

We did immediately learn the name of the United's only late-night waiter. *Gus* was sewn in raveling red thread on a breast pocket. He seemed as antique to us as any pseudo-Gothic or Federalist building on a Yale quad. Stooped and flat-footed, he wore an expression, bored, world-weary, or both, as he took our orders, turning an ear,

Such Dancing as We Can

presumably the better one, to each speaker in his turn. No one asked for the Baseball Special after all.

At last Gus gathered up the coffee-stained menus and waddled back to the kitchen. The old man wrote down none of our varied requests, and I marveled, thinking he must be a real pro, what my dad meant by an old-time waiter.

Gus soon returned with a tray of food that he stuck unceremoniously in the middle of the table for us to sort out. None of it bore the least resemblance to anything we'd asked him for, but for whatever reason, nobody thought to complain.

The week just past in New Haven had held other novel experiences for me. During Convocation, famed art historian Vincent Scully, the kind of spellbinding speaker I'd never heard, assured our class that we represented a thousand future world leaders. I instantly concluded that the description couldn't possibly apply to me, and, looking around at the other 900-plus freshmen, I likewise remember having my doubts.

Fifty-odd years later, my inference still feels right. In the case of those who did become leaders, it was, with a few honorable exceptions, as big-money men, not moral, intellectual, or cultural exemplars. It was if the arts and humanities had been youthful hobbies, abruptly abandoned once financial goals appeared on the horizon. For all its cheerleading about liberal education, this was the Ivy League way.

On the day after Convocation, I was far more taken by Professor Scully's class lecture. His was my first-ever art history course, starting with classical sculpture and architecture and ending, at year's end, with the modern abstract painters. There in the United, if I squinted my eyes, I could almost make the images of Greek monuments on the diner's murals into those of Mr. Scully's slides.

I did a lot of such squinting that year, because for all my greenhorn irony, I enjoyed being imaginatively transported in that or any way.

My daily schedule at the beginning of college days was about exactly opposite to the one I'd adopt for the far greater part of my life afterwards. Once I moved on from lowly freshman status, I'd gotten most of my required courses out of the way and could choose ones that met in the afternoon or, at worst, at 11 a.m., which allowed me to sleep in. So far as a true education was concerned, this scarcely represented a good premise for selection.

Such Dancing as We Can

As a freshman, however, I couldn't duck those morning classes, including ones on Saturday, and as soon as the last was dismissed, I would usually return to bed. On awakening from my nap, I'd think of something to amuse myself until suppertime. Sadly enough, alcohol– a demon I was later greatly aided in exorcising, praise be– played a progressively prominent part in such amusement, more, say, than hockey practice, swims at the gym, or studies.

My schoolwork waited until after dinner, and it often took me well into the early hours of the next day. I soon, therefore, became more or less a habitué of the United, going there for a break at least three times a week, sometimes in company, more often on my own.

I suspect every college freshman at some point tries to dope out a schedule that will allow him (we were all hims at early-sixties Yale) somehow to beat the system. Most of my friends soon discovered there was no such magic formula and went back to saner behavior. I either failed to make that discovery myself, or, having made it, persisted no matter. I honestly can't remember which.

Becoming a regular led to frequent contact with Spiro, the diner's proprietor, a soulful-visaged Greek who dressed, invariably, in blue suit and solid dark tie. He assigned himself the night shift at the register because, as I shortly discovered, he had another enterprise in the daytime.

I'd sometimes be the only customer in the wee hours, so after about three weeks of showing up at Spiro's establishment, I was let into a confidence. He stressed that I was not to share it with anyone. The man's chief ambition, it turned out, was to complete the epic poem he'd long been working on, *Sixty Steps from Yale.* He'd accumulated more than seventy pages of manuscript, all of them in Greek, and all composed, he claimed, in genuinely Homeric measure.

Spiro had cultivated a manner of discussing his undertaking in a sort of book-jacket argot. *Sixty Steps from Yale,* he announced, was a tale at once sweet and dark, sorrowful and uplifting. It concerned a beautiful Greek girl, recently arrived in America, and a Yale student from an old Connecticut family. The two had fallen in love.

Spiro would insert a Byronic hand between shirt and jacket front, lean his head back, and proceed more or less like this. "The young Greek woman is of humble origins but of noble spirit. She meets her lover at her father's restaurant. He catches her eye from his table. How great is the distance that separates them, yet how much greater the attraction that instantly blooms in their hearts."

I don't quote Spiro exactly, I'm sure, but I do catch his manner. "The couple's destiny is written in heaven," he might begin, "but everything on earth seems to interfere with it. The boy's parents disapprove, the girl's are annoyed by the Yale man's airs. At times wildly comic, at others gloomy, *Sixty Steps from Yale* is a love story, but also a look at two cultures, one ancient and one young."

His English was every bit as articulate and high-flown as I suggest.

Sixty years later, I wince at how I betrayed my pledge of secrecy. The very day after I promised confidence, I shared what I'd heard with my closest companions. I aped the old man's blurbese, and my cohort obligingly guffawed.

I know now that I should instead have felt honored by Spiro. There seems to have been something in me, specifically, that he considered congenial, perhaps even poetic, no matter that the notion of my becoming a poet would have struck me as absurd in those day. No, I liked booze, girls, and ice hockey, in descending order of preference. I certainly had no epic intentions, no ambition as a writer of any kind, none in fact as anything. I'd instinctively rejected Professor Scully's prognostications of my future.

As a sophomore, I moved farther away from where I'd been billeted that first year. My schedule hadn't become much saner, and yet my sorties to the United became ever rarer. The Connecticut drinking age being 21, I'd befriended a local dry cleaner, who served as my liquor dealer until graduation. Now my late-night diversions tended to involve nothing *but* liquor, until my trips to the United ceased altogether.

Thus it was at least a year after it happened that I learned of Spiro's death– and only because my eye was accidentally caught by an obituary in the New Haven *Register*. No mention, alas, of his epic, which, I assumed, remained unfinished. I surmised it would never be discovered, save, perhaps, by some family member, who'd stash it away or discard it along with other keepsakes from the writer's life. I recall a real pang to consider that.

I'm older than Spiro in those days, even older, I'd guess, than our waiter Gus, who back then struck us as so unimaginably aged.

Unlike those two, I find no orthodoxy, Greek or otherwise, fitted to my beliefs. And yet just this morning, prompted who-knows-how, I found myself praying, and scarcely for the first time, that God might forgive me for having once shown qualities so often conjoined in the young– stupidity and arrogance.

How, after all, can I know that *Sixty Steps from Yale* was fit for ridicule? I never read it, of course, having, in Ben

Jonson's words, small Latin, less Greek. Still, with all the confidence of an immitigable ignorance, I imagined the work to be ridiculous, sentimental, overwrought.

Unlike poor Spiro, I've published sixteen collections of poetry. I've won a prize or two, garnered this or that sweetheart fellowship, taught in various higher educational institutions (Yale among them) for over four decades. I was my state's Poet Laureate a few years back and have since received its most prestigious arts award.

At the same time, of course, I remain a stranger to the vast majority of citizens, bookish ones included, even within tiny Vermont. After I'm gone, my obscurity will in all likelihood become as complete as Spiro's. The diner itself lives only in the sketchy memories of alumni of my vintage and older. With no false humility, I can say that I'll lack the sort of accomplishment that its owner could have pointed to. After all, he did manage his restaurant for a long time, and well.

Perhaps I'm the sentimental one these days, but now it strikes me that there was real poetry in Spiro's merely composing what he did of *Sixty Steps from Yale,* given his need to keep his establishment going, to keep Gus and his daytime colleagues content, to keep serving what was, after all, pretty decent food. As I recall all this, it seems that Spiro's very authorial effort was epic in and of itself.

Sydney Lea

SUNYA

In my many years of education, apart from the most basic arithmetic I could never quite grasp anything that involved numbers. I still struggle on that score. I recall the words of Mr. Dunham, the very best teacher in my entire school, or so I was told. "Let's face it, son, you'll never be a mathematician."

As if I didn't know that.

What in this world, I wondered, did Rick and Teddy, the algebra hotshots, *see* as they blithely and swiftly dug up the ineffable X?

A certain venerable pine tree was another matter entirely. All the while I was there, it stood in the courtyard, valiantly fending off some sickness, though over time its limbs crashed one by one to earth. I knew that pine very well. Come late spring semester, it always held a robin and her downy chicks, and I watched them, rapt, maybe because, like the old tree that housed them, the birds embodied survival.

I could see a tree and some birds, and beyond, clouds that I squinted at, trying to force one or the other, before it drifted into nonexistence, to resemble something I could identify, though the effort rarely proved successful. But calculus, physics, economics? Don't ask me a thing. I ducked all but the latter in college, and economics therefore became the one course I failed in those four years. My clearer impressions from that course also came through a window in a fetid classroom.

Back then, the Yale campus's beeches seemed immortal, their barks smooth, not pocked by disease as so many of their kind have since become. Squirrels assembled, somehow always a trio, in the beech nearest the room where I sat bemused. A pair would chase a solitary, after which they'd rotate, as if they understood the notion of *it* from playground tag, though no twosome ever caught a single.

They seemed to be having fun, as I was emphatically not.

No, I was only baffled. What, just for one instance, had that New York City whiz encountered in his life that emboldened him to challenge our professor over some assertion, which I surely didn't understand even then? I could never own any knowledge unless I could integrate it with some personal experience. That's true to this day.

I had a good friend in the class— he'd later teach law— but he sat as far from me as possible in that third-story cell, as if he might catch my ineptitude like an airborne virus. He's gone now, like nearly half the classmates who traveled with me through these places I recall. In due course, we'll be down to zero.

Zero: I've always considered that one easy enough to grasp. By chance, however, I lately read that no one did grasp it until a Hindu mathematician named Brahmagupta proved the zero to have null value, something that he referred to as *sunya*. Apparently, that indicates *empty of any intrinsic nature,* a notion that itself eludes me. How can there be such a thing?

Just before I graduated from high school, my sickly pine was hewn and, as the last college year ebbed, my beech had started to scar. No squirrels used it anymore.

Such Dancing as We Can

II Bright Ambush

Sydney Lea

EARTHQUAKES AND ANGELS

So there I was, training again for a flat-water kayak race near our beloved camp in Washington County, Maine. August of 2016, a great interlude in my life: I was 73, but to churn the water for five miles in fifty-odd minutes, and to feel strong enough meanwhile that I could notice the lavish splendors of the neighborhood– well, it all but gave me the illusion that I'd never grow truly old.

I could maintain racing speed at the same time as I noted, say, a cow and calf moose plunging their heads into Picnic Cove for its spatterdock. I'd hear loons shriek when eagles soared into sight, so great a bane has the resurgence of these raptors proven to their young. One evening, the wind entirely in my favor, I passed within yards of a young coyote as it drank from Oxbrook Lake. Waterborne, I could dream that those landlubber deerflies and mosquitoes were mere figments of fancy.

The race was canceled for fear of lightning. A good thing, maybe, because two weeks after its scheduled date I had a heart attack. Insofar as my symptoms didn't closely resemble any I'd ever read or heard about, when I visited the tiny clinic on the New Brunswick border, the nearest facility to our remote cabin, I was more than surprised when the blood test indicated ischemia. Within a few hours, I'd arrive by ambulance at Bangor's medical center

Such Dancing as We Can

to have a stent placed in my occluded right coronary artery.

Three weeks thereafter, I found myself in rehab, pedaling a stationary bike and hauling on a rowing machine, keeping my heart rate near 120 or so for three quarters of an hour at a time, feeling better than I had when I didn't know there was anything wrong with me except for a geezer's occasional stiff back and his ever more creaky knees.

Almost exactly a year after my crisis, I entered the 2017 race and came in third. Of course a win would have been more gratifying; on the other hand, the ages of the two men who beat me, combined, amounted to less than my own, and I established a personal best for the course.

I was a lucky fellow, and am.

One reason for my adopting a passion over a decade ago for the two-bladed paddle lay, precisely, in the degeneration of my knees. For a few years, with the aid of plenty of Tylenol and the occasional cortisone shot, I could still hike reasonably well, but less and less could I do so with the unmixed pleasure of older times. I began to practice the kayak regime, which entails no impact, ever more avidly.

Again, there's the benefit that, especially when there's a bit of covering breeze, my progress remains quiet enough for me to witness all manner of natural wonders. I'll never forget the eagle that, as I plied the Connecticut River here in Vermont, stooped so hard onto a Canada goose that the poor bird might have been shot: a faint quiver or two, and then utter stillness. As the predator tore at the corpse, ravens drifted into the cottonwoods, waiting their turns– patient, soundless. I recall thinking, scarcely for the first time, *How do they know?* They always do, almost immediately. Uncanny.

Black bear and black duck. Otter and osprey. Beaver and bittern. Nighthawk and newt. Teal and turtle. I could go on.

My thoughts here, however scattered, may well be motivated by the notion of new knees, the first replacement slated for ten days from the time of recording all this. At my sanest, I'm aware how fortunate I've been, particularly as a lover of the outdoors, to live how and where I do, and thus, again and again, even as my undercarriage has made fun of me, to witness so many wonders, natural and otherwise. I also understand the advantages of existing in a medical era when procedures

Such Dancing as We Can

like the one I face have become pretty routine. Lord, nowadays the medicos can actually *print* your joint replacement by way of a computer command! And the stent inside me now might have saved my beloved father, dead of a coronary at 56.

At my most loathsomely self-pitying, though, I mope like a convict facing life. I moan about the imminent operations, and even more about the time that recovery will take, much greater than the program following my heart attack. My wife reminds me that I'll be paddling as hard as I want to before I take vigorous hikes again, but that the hikes will come too. Yet I maunder.

Some believe God sends them signs. I don't automatically reject the notion, feeling that I too have gotten signs from somewhere at crucial moments in my life. (Sadly, these are frequently ones I don't recognize except in retrospect.) I object to claims of supernatural guidance only when they evidence a disgraceful self-regard. I remember from some years back, for example, what a certain American pop star told an interviewer after he'd survived an earthquake in Japan that killed thousands. The disaster, he proclaimed, was the Almighty's way of telling him he'd been touring too much.

Sydney Lea

Of course. That must have been it...

That I like this twerp's music has taxed my ethics for what seems ages: I listen to his tunes even as my contempt for him abides. I should govern my judgment, though. Too often I've let myself be caught up in my *own* solipsism. How can I forget that intervention saved my life two years ago, and that modern medicine will more than likely enable me to climb the Green and White Mountains again, at however modest a pace?

Just recently I heard from my oldest friend on earth, a man I love and can't remember not knowing. He has stage three tongue cancer. This is a person who has been a model of healthful behavior: careful diet, no tobacco, very moderate liquor, all but obsessive exercise.

"It's not fair!" I shouted, for all the world like a five-year-old, into the receiver.

"Whatever happens, it's been a good life," Jimmy responded. Then, to my surprise, he broke into a lusty laugh. I felt as if he'd slapped me. Why, yes, why hadn't I thought of that? It *has* been good– every bit as much for me as for him, maybe even more so. He married a fine woman indeed, but he did so too late to enjoy parenthood. With his reaction as our cue, Jimmy and I shared some further laughter, thinking back on

Such Dancing as We Can

monkeyshines from the course of our long-shared coexistence.

You should know –this will prove relevant– that I'm two-finger typing as I write these words. Because this pal's father was a prison warden, I never learned to use a keyboard properly, some white-collar inmate always looking for ways to be on the warden's good side. Happily, that involved typing papers for his son. Because we were closest schoolmates, my own work came along for the ride.

In our tenth-grade year, though, we were getting nervous, since the embezzler who'd been serving us since middle school was about to get sprung. And then my buddy came in one morning, bouncing like a puppet. A forger had just been admitted. We were saved! Jimmy had vetted the new prisoner and reported that he, an even better typist than his predecessor, would be at our service right through graduation.

Now as it happened, this forger set about rehabilitating himself by making greeting cards– the whole deal, artwork *and* verse. Not so long after his arrival at the joint, the warden underwent a gall bladder operation, providing our bard a first opportunity to put his skills to the test.

A day or so later, Jimmy came in with his début effort. The front of the card looked quite professional. As a forger, after all, the fellow had some skill as a draftsman; but the stanza inside read as follows:

> *Sad to hear that you're sick.*
> *Hope it's just for a spell.*
> *Would love to come see you,*
> *But can't very well.*

We chuckled at some length over the memory. On hanging up, I felt instructed by my beloved chum, as I need to be by whomever else, that humor is among the very best ways of spitting into mortality's face.

Sam is another friend and a formidable poet, who quite some time ago lost his young wife to cancer. More recently, as if that caused him insufficient suffering, he was diagnosed with stage four cancer himself. He endured a robotic proctectomy, but there were apparently some gross medical blunders in the procedure. (Can one tongue-lash a robot? Perhaps not yet. I can't say I look forward to the time when one might.) He lapsed into renal failure and sepsis at his Connecticut apartment, where he was living alone. When he failed to answer phone calls for two days, one of his daughters made a call from New York to the Hartford police, exhorting them to break her father's door down.

Sam has since written to me that, after emerging from coma, he beheld that daughter and her sister sitting beside him in intensive care. He claims to have seen light rising behind their torsos in the shape of angels' wings, and I trust his testimony. My friend has known angelic intercession, and I have too. I recall that something like an aura surrounded my wife after that stent was installed, and that I thought, exactly, *She looks like an angel.* She was the fair one of our bogus Sunday school texts; his were African; but all three were angels, yes.

I need to remember how divine energies can manifest themselves in people who care about us. This poet friend's daughters are good for that. And needless to say, so is my life partner.

But what has been manifested to some other friends? How will any laugh again, as Jimmy and I did? Who will play the role of that poet's daughters for those bereft of children? How in God's name, for instance, does Robert avoid pure madness?

Robert. He's another pal from school days, though the word *pal* won't quite fit itself around someone like him. Back then, he was, well, eccentric. I suppose he still is. In our teen years, he dressed as somberly and formally as an undertaker, and while the rest of us boys had the typical obsessions of witless, hormone-driven adolescents, he had keen interests in contemporary poetry, art, and music. He also commanded an extraordinary awareness of the local and national political scenes, to which his classmates paid little if any attention.

Needless to say, he experienced a degree of bullying in those days; but while I could hardly claim to be a saint with regard to my own treatment of peers, somehow I always felt drawn to Robert and I stood up for him, even if he did a fair job of that on his own. The two of us see each other almost never, but we have stayed in touch for six decades.

Just recently I learned of the death, at 44, of his older daughter. I knew she'd had cancer. Bad enough: but this calamity followed a few years on the death by suicide of her younger sister.

How does Robert get up in the morning?

At school, he could recite the names and party affiliations not only of every U.S. senator but also of every U.S.

representative. That Hawaii and Alaska had not yet swollen the ranks of states to fifty scarcely alters the breadth of that old accomplishment. I remember how our feisty, gifted teacher Dan Charles marveled at this trick of Robert's, wondering why a young man with so capacious a mind could never pass his history course for want of completing written assignments.

In a chat with Robert many years later, I recalled Mr. Charles's puzzlement, and reflected on the fact that, brilliant as he indisputably was, the boy failed to make the cut anywhere but at an arts college. Now that school was reputable, to say the least, but somehow it proved unendurable to the young painter before a single semester had elapsed, and not for any lack of promise on his part.

It was then that Robert revealed something to me, which had been revealed to *him* in his fifties. He spoke of attending an off-Broadway play whose male lead had Asperger's Syndrome. "Halfway through the first act," he told me, "I said to myself, 'So *that's* it.'"

It's not that Robert had a less than respectable career. He wrote classical albums' liner notes for a spell; he was the classical music host for Minnesota Public Radio; he continued with his artwork and still does; but most of his professional life was devoted to the American Friends Service Committee, and involved extended residences in Moscow, among other intriguing things. Still he has a self-dismissive bent. While I regard him as the very epitome of aplomb, a person who has always marched to his own drummer, Robert frequently describes himself as a failure.

Among his regrets is to have neglected to pursue a gifted high school girl whom we both knew well, and who felt real attraction to his sensibility, his intellectual and artistic endowments, and indeed to his every idiosyncrasy. Robert ruefully describes her as his road not taken. He married another woman, saw the marriage gutter, but cherished his relationships with his three children– two of them now gone.

I recall my mother's saying that the worst part of growing old lay not in her personal challenges, mental and physical, but in the death, misfortune, and degeneration of so many priceless friends. I understand that very clearly now, the list of my own dear companions' woes seeming infinitely extensible as of late.

Will is another wonderful poet, whom I came to know, esteem, and cherish forty-plus years ago, after a poem of his won a poetry competition at *New England Review,* the quarterly I founded and edited. He and his wife are now grieving parents too, having very lately lost one of their three sons to the cursed opioid epidemic. He assures me I cannot imagine what that loss feels like, and no doubt he's exactly right. There's winter in my soul as I contemplate such misery, even in the abstract.

Yes, I need to be taught and re-taught that, should I drop in my tracks right now, I'll have had what the valiant Jimmy calls a good life, and then some. The fates of Robert and Will and Sam are acute reminders of this, though God strike me dead should I take any of these disasters as merely useful to me.

I recall the day that my wife and I attended a class for people with scheduled joint replacements, and for their caregivers. The nurse who delivered the segment on the surgery itself was clearly competent and well trained; but he gilded no lilies. I am farther from squeamish than many, yet even the hand-drawn illustrations he projected daunted me. The physical therapist proved a similarly no-nonsense type: she too exuded competence; she too emphasized the effort and time that rehabilitation would demand, and the inevitability of pain.

The weather outside the classroom was suitably dreary on that second day of March. Some hybrid of snow and rain slid down the plate glass windows, on the other side of which lay an unrelievedly drab landscape. Diminutive humans several stories below left blurry trails in the slush. These men and women, both the well and the infirm, struck me as doomed– just like me.

I thought of none of the close friends to whom I just referred in my catalog of catastrophes. I was too intent on how perfect a setting I'd found for my melancholic reverie. I should have seen that I was already a lucky man. In a sense, I could have looked at my looming operations as divine remonstrance. I began by mocking the vanity of a pop star, who saw that Japanese earthquake in a similar light– and my mood that afternoon was on the same continuum.

The earthquake I dodged in 2016, the year of my coronary, looks trivial as I consider the collective, seismic disasters encountered by some of my companions. If I further apply the labored metaphor to my own life, I'd say my most threatening earthquake comprised too many years of addiction, too many years when I was a mere vessel for the substances that sustained my psychic life– until they almost destroyed it.

This, I know, makes for abrupt closure. But the private enormity of dependence is the subject of another essay. Or perhaps, thank God, it will remain so vast as forever to lie beyond my rendering.

In any case, the main thing I must cleave to is this: looking back across years in which Jimmy and Robert and Sam and Will and a legion of others have hovered in my mental atmosphere, yes, like angels; looking back at enslavement to my compulsion; looking back near and far and deep, I must try to remember something utterly crucial.

One miracle a day ought to hold me.

TRAIL TO TOMORROW

My wife and I were snowshoeing in mid-February along the so-called Trail to Tomorrow, not far from our cabin in Maine, when she spotted an odd-looking lump some fifty feet back in the brush. With mittened hands and a windfall branch, we managed to excavate a pair of moose skulls, nose to nose. Rodents had gnawed the palms to nubs, but enough remained intact that we could easily recreate the scene. Two rutting bulls had locked antlers.

How slow and gruesome the animals' deaths must have been! If not for random misfortune, the larger one would have run the other off in short order. At all events, but for some bruises and scrapes, both would have gone on living. So it struck me– scarcely for the first time– how profoundly life can depend on simply dodging ill luck, and not always by way of our own caution.

Sydney Lea

We were feeling pretty lucky just then simply to have dodged the year's pervasive and lethal corona virus, at least up to that point. It was also a year of righteous rage in the nation's cities, indeed of ethnic strife all over the planet. And gushing glaciers, ruinous drought, ungovernable wildfire– these were not transient matters. Not at all.

Even if half-consciously, for my wits' sake I tend to repress the naked truth that, like the rest of earth's creatures, regardless of their historical moment, I confront forces far larger than I can conceive. I distract myself from them, as I suspect most humans do, by concentrating on the existences of those closest to me, and needless to say, on my own.

I think of a moment last spring, for example, when I was clearing our pond's standpipe of debris piled around it by beavers. One rough stick turned out to be the tail of a snapping turtle. What if I'd grabbed its other end? I wouldn't have died, but you see what I mean. I still shiver to think about it.

And my blood freezes whenever I recall how years back my wife was late one day to pick up our youngest daughter from nursery school. A good thing too. They came around a curve on the way home and saw a crumpled car on its side. A great orange gash flashed from a wayside pine, torn by the dead boy in the wreckage, who mere seconds before had spun across the very road my wife and daughter were taking.

How different life would feel today if they'd been on time.

Last fall, after I'd passed a car on the Interstate and was checking the mirror before I steered back, my wife blurted, "Get in the right lane!" Within mere seconds, some bonehead's car, traveling south on the northbound road, whizzed by.

Our family's intact, and not caged somewhere, not trying to shelter from bombs. We're assured of food, and only because we are blessed, not cursed, by where we were born and in what condition. Luck.

Surely the weaker moose died first, and for him, that was actually a version of good fortune too. Just think of how the stronger one dragged his antagonist's corpse around until exhaustion undid him.

We carried the two blanched skulls back to our camp, where we scrubbed them clean and nailed them over the woodshed door as… Well, what on earth to call them?

Sydney Lea

Icons?

Perhaps, though I can't say of what.

Such Dancing as We Can

SHORT SAD STORY

As he pushed open the door of room 116 at the Longhorn Motel, I noticed the stranger's befuddled grin. "Oh, this is–" he mumbled, trailing off, backing out. I had hours to wait before I flew back east from nearby Denver, so, seated at a chipped Formica table, I'd been trying, with small success, to rough out a piece of writing. As if it would help my efforts, I locked the door against further distractions, even benign ones like this petty mistake.

A few minutes later, however, the knob began to rattle. I slid the bolt. "What's the matter?" I snapped when I saw the same man standing there. "Can't you read numbers? *One-One-Six.* That's me, not you." The other didn't appear to hear. He leaned against the door with one shoulder, cradling an ill-sorted bunch of clothes in both hands.

"Get the hell out of here!" I snapped, because he started directly to lean against *me*. The interloper was a younger but smaller man than I. Putting my forearms against his chest, I shoved him hard, so that he fell outside onto the lot's asphalt, a plaid pajama top flying one way, a gravy-stained shirt the other, and a sock landing over both eyes like a flimsy blindfold. Even masked, his face wore that silly smile. It might have been a comical sight otherwise. I relocked my door.

My writing continued to go nowhere at all, so, in spite of the time gaping before me, I decided to repack my own clothes. Then I shaved, though I really didn't need to. I couldn't make those minor chores last long, however, and soon I headed for the lobby to grab a cup of coffee from the motel's vending machine. On my way, I spotted the erratic fellow once more. He was up on his feet at the very spot where I'd bowled him over, his odd bundle of garments regathered, the smile still showing, though not directed at anyone or anything in particular, least of all at the one who'd shoved him.

I asked the desk clerk. "What the hell's the story with that guy?"

"Seems like he's lost," the clerk answered. "I gave him the key to room 124, but he keeps tellin' me he needs to get into 116."

"My room," I mused, obviously.

"I figure he's drunk as a skunk," the clerk snarled, turning brusquely back to his affairs.

Such Dancing as We Can

I went out for breakfast, dawdling for more than an hour over my meal and small talk with the sweet, grandmotherly waitress at a beanery called The Country Fare. When I returned to the Longhorn, I found the showroom-clean, white Ford 150 still parked in front of 116, but its owner was nowhere to be seen. I stepped into the motel lobby again.

"What became of our friend?" I asked. The clerk said he'd found him in some other room, not 116 but not 124 either, the room he'd been assigned. Apparently, all he could say was, "I'm waiting for my daughter."

In the end, not knowing what else to do, the clerk had called the police. In due course, the cops summoned the EMTs.

I don't know what happened after that, because I left for my flight, much earlier than I needed to. On the way to the airport in the rental car, seated by the gate, airborne, and all through the long drive northward to Vermont after touchdown, I couldn't help feeling rotten about having heaved that guy onto his backside. I understood why guilt might bother me as it did; but I couldn't quite sort out the other ways I felt. I tried to console myself, of course. How, after all, could I have known that the trespasser was not of sound mind?

Yet almost a year later, I still sense that same mix of guilt and whatever else may be. If anything, my trouble of spirit has strengthened, broadened, as if it may last me lifelong. Perhaps at least I can write about it. Maybe I *have* always written about it in some vague way. Whatever it is.

I remember arriving at our house that night, dog-tired in body and heart, and, right after supper with my wife, going up to bed; but a more powerful memory is of a dream I had some time toward dawn, in which that lovely wife stood by me and the second of our three daughters beside a bonfire we'd lit at the end of our woodlot road. A quiet bliss pervaded the vision, or rather a feeling like the peace that the apostle Paul describes, *which passeth all understanding.*

For a moment, still pretty much asleep, I guess, I arrived at the warming conclusion that such peace might actually remain in the world even after I left it, and that somehow it could be available to any person sufficiently needing it. Coming to, I felt desolate to recognize my fantasy as just that.

There had been times when I needed such peace for myself, and there would be other times to come. I knew

Such Dancing as We Can

as much. I hoped it would be accessible again, though I understood I couldn't simply will it into being.

I didn't think of the smiling man at the Longhorn right away, though now I realize I might have.

Sydney Lea

BRIGHT AMBUSH

Fats Domino and Little Richard changed my generation's musical tastes. Though he was no hero of mine, Elvis ripped off their r&b groove and had even greater success. But before all that, I'd ached for Patti Page, "The Singin' Rage," as the deejays dubbed her. I remember loving "Mockingbird Hill" and "Tennessee Waltz," and though I now recognize "How Much Is that Doggie in the Window?" as supremely corny, in my middle teens it touched my heart. I'd stare for minutes on end at Patti's picture on an LP album I owned.

Toward the end of her life, that star somehow fell on New Hampshire, just across the river from where we live. Her housekeeper is a friend of ours, and back when I told her that Ms. Page had sold more records in the '50s than any other female singer, she was stunned. But then I suspect that eight out of ten of my neighbors– and all of them younger, say, than 75– would give me blank looks if I mentioned Patti's name. They'd no doubt be like the looks that Audrey Wurdemann would evoke, even from career writers, if I were to name her now, though she won the 1935 Pulitzer Prize in poetry for her volume, *Bright Ambush*.

Such Dancing as We Can

Tatters and shards. "Nothing beside remains." That's how a more enduring poet, Percy Shelley, described the condition of the fallen King Ozymandias.

If one let it, this all could be deeply depressing.

Well, go that way if you choose. For my part, a sense of reputation's fickleness frees me, having just changed a grandson's diaper, to celebrate. The brightness of the child's very body waste, however improbably, may lead me to a paean of some sort.

Just now, however, I notice– with a catch in my breath, with a rage to sing about them, even if there's no one to listen– spring's thousand thousand greens, come back to swathe our hills.

Sydney Lea

MICAH, WEEPING, 1978

On Memorial Day, or Decoration, as village elders still called it, McClure's Student Band played taps and the flag was lowered to half-staff. I noticed Micah the plumber weeping.

The Vietnam War, over four decades past now, seemed three years dead and gone even then– to me, at least. Lord, I should have learned *something* by '78. A college roommate had been blown to pieces out there in '64, after all. That was in the era of American "advisers," before very few even knew where Vietnam lay.

My friend's death had gotten me going in the non-stop '60s protest happening. I'll tell you what: if we couldn't have found the "enemy" on a map, we sure as hell knew how to party. I'll tell you what too: we were full of crap, not merely about the war but a host of other things.

Well, maybe not full, but at least half.

My friends and I turned 80 this year. Those who remain, that is. But even at 36, I should have been a lot more sensitive than I was, inwardly sneering at our small town's tradesman, slumped on the village common, his shameless tears losing themselves in his multiple chins.

Such Dancing as We Can

I shouldn't have jeered him, even silently: *Fat, goofy Micah and his whiskey-tears!* I pictured him popping his khaki trousers, the seams blowing out of his army-issue shirt.

I should have had other things to imagine, of course. I get that now and should have then, but no one had shot at me, so I found it too easy to think that Micah just looked loopy, his cap dribbling down his head like a clump of snow off a roof.

I watched him askance as someone on the bandstand recited the bromides: *bravery, honor, duty, sacrifice.* He stood as erect as he could, weeping even more obviously.

Soon after that morning it was Micah's guts that exploded. Gunfire didn't kill him but booze did. And nowadays his namesake son, about the same age as his father on that day in '78, is always plastered himself.

Should Micah somehow show up today, I swear I'd have better words for him, if only– minus sardonic adjectives– his name.

Sydney Lea

AT MY AGE, I WHISTLE

George MacArthur was a great one for whistling through his teeth.

He was, however, more renowned for other things. During the autumn of 1929, for example, he cut railroad ties, or sleepers, as they were known here in the north country, out on Lake Wabassus, whose name local people have always shortened to "Wabass."

George made it a point to memorialize every significant season of his life and labor in song. He'd borrow a well-known tune for the melody, and string his own words upon it. That fall of '29 resulted in "The "Wabass Cannonball."

I remember each note and verse:

Listen to the jingle, the rumble and the roar;
You could hear the ice a-bucklin' up and down old Wabass shore.
When I arrived at old Wabass Lake, 'twas early in the fall,
And Belding's crew was glad to meet the Wabass Cannonball.
I asked Belding for a job, and he filled me wish surprise,
When he said "Go take your sleeper axe and start in makin' ties."
There was about a week and a half when the sun never shone at all,
The air was filled so full of chips by the Wabass Cannonball.
Then we went up to old Third Lake to have a little cheer,

Such Dancing as We Can

And drove the length of Slaughter Point to try and shoot a deer.
Well, the big buck came down Slaughter Point, and he had no horns at all,
'Cause his face was filled with buckshot by the Wabass Cannonball.
Then the warden came into our camp and they thought they had us beat,
For cooking in an iron pot they found a little meat.
Then they hauled us into court but they had no case at all,
And the both of them were BEAT TO HELL by the Wabass Cannonball!

I may know why I thought about all this at dawn last May, alone in my room at the Park Hotel, which overlooks lovely Lake Bled in Slovenia, even if this is a world about as far from Wabass as anyI could conjure. I was to give a talk that day at a literary conference, in which I'd been asked to answer at some length this question: Where do poems come from?

If I had been completely truthful, as I wasn't, I'd have answered by saying, "I don't really know." Fact is, poems just come. Or at least they used to. For the better part of my adulthood, they have simply been facts of life. I could say I learned as much from George: your experience brings you a poem– or not. Poems come– or they don't.

Sydney Lea

Their coming is rarer for me now than in prior days, and at times I worry that my own will to string words onto experience may have retreated, indeed may in due course vanish, even before I vanish myself. In any case, lately I often wake up with *others'* tunes in mind.

Then I whistle them all day.

George could test people's patience by the same habit: he whistled too, especially in hours of idleness, but at least the words in his head, I'm certain, belonged to him alone. I drive my poor wife to distraction with my all but tuneless whistling of compositions that have nothing to do with any creative spark of mine. It's almost as though I've surrendered proprietorship of my own language.

Of course I've gone through similar periods of self-doubt before; they just haven't been so protracted and unsettling.

Be all that as it may, I don't romanticize when I say that George had a substantial literary influence on me. And yes, if it sometimes seems that what remains to me is just a patch

on what my words once sought, if I can manage little but a less than birdlike song, this doesn't mean I love those worlds any less than once I did.

Such Dancing as We Can

This whistling is puny, and yet it's likely still a stab at making the various worlds I've known or heard about cohere, no matter that the deeper those worlds sink into memory, the shallower my breath, the thinner my tune.

Sydney Lea

STRANGER LOVE

Was that a boy or a grownup in the car next to mine? I couldn't guess his age.

When I got out, he reached through the passenger window and grappled my hand. "Hey!" he shouted "My name... my name... my name..." He squirmed, he stammered, he all but choked, his eyes suggesting agony. Clearly, his mind was off.

The manchild kept at his labored chant until the woman who drove him– mother? sister? keeper?– came around to where I stood and finished the sentence. "He says his name is Marcus." She gently parted our hands, having spoken more softly than I'd have predicted. Her behavior pleased me, as does any instance of human compassion, big or small, in these fraught days.

A Shih-Tzu sat calm as the Buddha in Marcus's lap.

"I'm glad to meet you," I said. "Is that your dog?"

His eyes rolled back.

"He's a good little guy," I went on, a bit over-urgently; but I did mean it. From what I've seen, that breed can be pretty yappy.

Such Dancing as We Can

"Are you the poet?" his cheerful companion asked me.

Taken aback, I aimed at self-dismissal: "Well, one of the many."

There's no particular creed in my private beliefs, but I do give weight to grace, or *chesed,* as Judaism calls it, the notion that gratuitous favor can be visited on anyone.

I have three dogs of my own that I cherish, for minimal instance. More importantly, as I've said again and again in these pages, I could pray for no better wife, and five beloved children are sound and sane, as are their sons and daughters. What have I really done to deserve their cherished affection? Call all this whatever you want; I call it a godsend.

I looked up at the newspaper rack on the store's front porch: even from fifteen feet off, the headlines showed boldly. The latest mass shooting, depleted state and federal budgets, one more war somewhere.

What will ever save us? Some, it's claimed, cast off their crutches at Lourdes. I've seen signs and wonders, but none so spectacular.

"*I love you!*" Marcus bawled as his driver backed onto the road.

Sydney Lea

The Couple at the Free Pile

Autumn's church bazaar was over, all the stalwart, weathered tents of the vendors struck except the one over the White Elephant table. Early that Sunday morning, such tatty wares as had gone unsold still sprawled on the plastic tablecloth or on the ground, but the sign up front read FREE.

No car approaching or following, I braked to a crawl so I could observe a man and woman making their deliberate ways through the jumble. I naturally noticed that their goods were gathered in the rusted bed of the wheelbarrow my wife and I had donated to the event, which nodded on its flat tire like a weary draft animal.

For me to stop completely might be to embarrass this couple, who coveted what we congregants had considered encumbrances. And yet, however it shames me now, my curiosity –like desperate thirst, or lust– also impelled me. I'd drive on, circle the village common, and pass back that way again from the other direction. After all, the two scavengers seemed devoted to their scrutinies; I doubted they'd notice my second inspection.

I turned by a picket fence enclosing a big house's tidy lawn at the south end of the common. The owners held a well-attended garden tour there last June. Then I swung right again, north, going by the famous corner elm, which residents agreed at town meeting to save, approving a line item that funded the tree surgeons' services.

During the festival, I'd visited the White Elephant booth myself. As the saying goes, one man's trash is another man's treasure, and you never know. As I predicted, however, nothing appealed. Among other bits of uselessness, say, I found a basketball so worn it had lost all traces of its original, pebbled orange; three recumbent, saucer-eyed ceramic deer; a few chipped plates, inscribed *Disneyland, 1974* and showing portraits of Goofy, Donald, and other cartoon figures. There were unraveling rugs, tarnished lampshades and sconces, so on.

Passing the elementary school, I made a right again, and, before the turn that would take me to another view, I stopped at the intersection, just opposite the village store. A friend of mine and I would be having lunch there in an hour or so. Its deli is the best-stocked one for miles, the staff all cheerful.

As I drove, even more slowly than before, past the White Elephant display, I saw a car seat in a Bondo'd pickup's cab. It held a child, and he or she –it was hard to tell through the windows' grime– must have been sleeping a few minutes before, but now I could just make out a mouth, gaped in a yowl I couldn't hear, even if I could imagine it. Surely one of the parents, or both, would go tend the toddler. For now, though, they stood motionless, one on either side of the wheelbarrow, eyes on me. Their stares were furious.

Such Dancing as We Can

SLOW ON THE UPTAKE

The corona virus shut down my paddle races in 2020. Just as well. I'm talking about the races, Lord knows, not the virus. In middle June, I'd had an operation on my right hand, one designed to rectify a botched earlier carpal tunnel procedure. I was cautioned to treat my thumb and first two fingers delicately for six weeks, so I'd never have gotten in shape for the twelve-miler scheduled for early August. But there'd be other races in other places.

Immediately after my first post-surgical workout on our beloved Maine lake, my wife took a picture of me. One of our granddaughters saw it and said, *Look! Grandpa's smiling!* My face was contorted, yes. I wasn't smiling.

I can dwell on doom sometimes, not blessings like the sweet child's own unique and beautiful smile. Like how on whitecap days such as that one the west wind striates the surface with parallel lines of foam. Like the half-grown eagle that struck the water's surface twice, fishing its way to a tree, from which it now screamed.

I idled below the big raptor's perch. I needed the break, though I lied to myself that I just wanted to check on its fortunes. They had been less than mine. I saw that I should feel privileged simply to be there, rocking side to side.

Tax your old muscles and bones like this, I told myself, every day if you can, as strenuously as you can. Extend your years as far as possible. But I was an old man now, and Mother Nature would remain undefeated. I'd be gone before long, the way new grass withers and dies– a notion from Scripture, which may mean nothing to you. That's none of my business.

My die-hard spirit dies hard, but after that snapshot was taken, it struck me that a month without exercise would have weakened anyone, even a young man. As my mother used to say when stubbornness blinded me to some obvious thing, *You're slow on the uptake, pal.*

I felt I had little time– and all the time in the world. I could be here now, as one 60s icon advised after he went from Harvard professor Richard Alpert to aspirant Buddhist monk Baba Ram Dass. I was in my twenties then.

I remember the would-be monk's father, a corporate lawyer, calling him "Baba Rum-Dumb." Even then, I shared some of that parent's cynicism, but staying in the present *is* a worthy aim. No, it won't free the poor and oppressed in our time any more than in Ram Dass's salad days and my own, for all our idealisms. Nor, to quote a song from that era, have we found the way we put an end to war. That's a truth we've been confirming and reconfirming since humans started to farm and, in the process, conceived of property.

I still long to demolish injustice, but at my age it's worth being diverted by what's left of wonders– like that salmon, bright as a jeweler's gem, fifteen feet deep in the cove beneath the eagle's perch, in water so clear I could look right through it, so pure I could drink it.

Sydney Lea

A Stranded Moose

Having stopped to tow a woman out of a mud-season ditch, I came home, kicked off my boots, and brewed a cup of coffee. Oh, how gallant I'd been. Oh, how easy my life is.

This roadside incident brought to mind a local moose's fix last fall. She'd stranded herself shoulder-deep in the bog at the southerly end of Long Pond. Of course, a car in the mud is one thing, a foundered moose another. One is a matter of inconvenience, the other of life or death. The animal was helpless, paralyzed.

Fish and Game officers came out with block and tackle but they couldn't even reach her. Should they have let nature take its course, as sentimentalists like to say? Not by my lights. It was a kindness to shoot that poor creature dead, leaving her there for the ravens.

I can almost hear the officers' words. "There's was nothing else we can do." I surmise a good deal of melancholy in that declaration.

Forget your Disney movies: the so-called course of nature is often, perhaps usually, cruel as can be. So yes, I'm glad that the moose didn't live on to drown in the muck. What a death. Instead, her great head dropped to the water, a hole behind each eye, her foot-long dewlap splayed among the pickerel weed. The dark, ever-garrulous birds started to gather right off.

Or so I say. I wasn't there. The only part of that moose I ever saw, a ribcage, came almost eight months later when I came to paddle the pond for what's called recreation. Now I recreate from some bones and from hearsay what I figure must have unfolded. How close am I to the truth? I haven't asked anyone. Something in me, you see, is always in search of a story, the more dramatic the better. Musing's often my muse, to give it a fancy name, and I don't like to have it curtailed.

Such a pompous inclination may simply display male egotism, a craving to play a role: hero, even begetter. Whatever you do, don't trust me.

I don't even trust myself as imagination gallops from one inventive move right on to another one. To choose something wholly at random, I may be driving along and the regular *thrups* of pavement seams will trigger a memory, maybe a bass drum's thump in a jazz club back in my twenties. And if it doesn't, who'll stop me here from saying it does?

Sydney Lea

THEY SEEM TO KNOW

Where did the burying beetles come from and how did they know that a truck had flattened a frog on our dirt road? Some call them carrion beetles. They're perversely pretty. With their tidy orange belts, you could take them for bumblebees. But rapacious? That poor frog vanished overnight.

The natural world can be downright uncanny. The bugs got me thinking of the trout we stock in our pond for local children and how, the minute we do, the predators gather: herons, mergansers, mink, and some we rarely see otherwise, like ospreys and, particularly lethal, otters. It's astonishing how quickly those fish can disappear but more astonishing that those creatures know to show up in the first place.

I remember hearing on our radio, maybe four years ago, about an almost biblical plague of grasshoppers somewhere in Utah. Once again, part of the report that seemed at least equally amazing was how farmers had to contend with another curse, the army of gulls that flew all the way from the coast to feed on the insects and befoul the fields. Or maybe they were inland gulls from the Great Plains. My power of recall is not what it was. It doesn't matter. Either way, those gulls were also a wonder. How did *they* know?

Such Dancing as We Can

The instinct that draws such creatures chills me. It's not that I'm squeamish, just self-absorbed, I suspect. I'm likely not the one to judge. And, of course, I can't begin to compare the epic to the personal. Still, there have been instances when I swear I foresaw some things as if by instinct, a number of them very much against my will: the car crash that would one day kill a good friend, say; or the Blue Jays defeating the Phillies in the '93 World Series; my father, although he looked healthy, destroyed in due course by his heart; my teenage girlfriend later losing interest in men; a bull at my uncle's farm getting ready to charge so I'd better get up a tree; on and on.

This all used to be a potpourri of dark and bright, inconsequential and tragic; but with passing years, such inklings tend to bring on the more ominous side almost exclusively. I suppose there's a logic to that. In any case, to shield myself from things I just don't *want* to predict, I come up with ways to distract myself when their threat looms.

After the frog was devoured, lying in bed that night I tried to think up some towns which I could match to countries whose opening letters they shared: Jericho, right here in Vermont, for instance, and Jordan. That diverted me into pondering how many nations begin with C but

just one apiece with O and Q and– needless to say– none
with X.

Well, so what? Well, I know what: these are mindless
efforts against gloom. That particular night I meant to
forget the beetles, or rather the way they stole in,
uncanny, from who-knows-where. Like so much else.

Such Dancing as We Can

SAME OLD PATH:
    –January 12, 2020

It's the anniversary of the 2010 Haitian earthquake, to which dear friends lost a son. That too was the day when a treasured former student of mine collapsed at 40 as he ran on the beach in Savannah. Congenital bad heart, it seems, though no one knew that until he was gone.

Here, in a landscape very different either from Haiti's or Georgia's, my dogs sniff some winter-killed animal ruin. Spring– that cliché– seems hard to envision.

I climb to stay fit as I can, choosing the same trails that the wild game uses. I like to read tracks in snow. Sometimes I make them first; sometimes the creatures do.

Surf raked a Georgia shoreline, hot wind clawed at a Haitian mountain, but late winter's perversely blue today as I make my way through the woods.

I want to shriek, *Come back!*

I stop where a brook runs under ice. I hear the hum, and say *Life is good*. But my mind's a spiral, so I know better than to liken this blather of water to song. I step long, not to break through.

How would *good* sound to parent or lover?

Sydney Lea

It's as if I've chosen this path I'm on, but anything with feet would take it. I have no special instinct.

I'm excited to see moose prints, so rare have the great creatures become because of the ever-burgeoning tick population. The size of its hooves might compare to headstones'....

No, no figure of speech stands up to grief.

I think, *we're only along for the ride,* however much we think we generate motion. I'm holding on for dear life, in fact– though I meant to follow something, and thought I'd be followed by something.

III Sunday Morning

Sydney Lea

My Tribe and I

In a characteristically compelling essay called "Grub: A Man in the Market,"[1] Garret Keizer briefly muses on his distaste for upper New England farmers' markets. He concedes that those institutions appeal to what his wife Kathy calls "our tribe." That's the tribe, I suppose, one might equally associate with me and my own wife, yet on reading Garret's essay, my inner Marianne Moore announced, right out loud, "I too dislike it," by which I seem to have meant tribe and market at once.

The spontaneity of my response surprised me; and it occasioned the following reflections on things and people I have historically liked. I'll get back to the farmers' market scene in due course, but for a spell I mean to remember some chapters of my life and the persons I most fondly associate with them.

My father's people, from Wiltshire, England, came to this country before it *was* a country. There were two Lea

---

[1] *1. "Grub: A Man in the Market,"* Raritan, *v. xxxvii, no. 3, winter 2018*

brothers; one set about farming in eastern Pennsylvania, the other in what became Tennessee. My mother's Mennonite ancestors, so called Pennsylvania Dutch, arrived more than a century later, and put down roots in Berks County.

As time went by, the Leas, while none gained true distinction (unless you count Annabelle, the wife whom Sam Houston abandoned when he lit out for Texas), attained a degree of gentility. This sank back to a shabbier sort as they approached the generation of my father's father. The Klines, my mother's forebears, fared markedly better: her bachelor uncle took his father's drugstore and in due course turned it into one of the most profitable prescription pharmaceutical companies in the nation. That uncle was the soul of the German Reform version of Protestant ethic, minus the religion, to which in fact he was unabashedly hostile.

My mother may have coveted some of the accrued plumminess of the Lea name, however lapsed to lesser luster, so as to ballast what she perhaps regarded as bumpkin's heritage on the Berks County side. I say this with some compunction, because after all her husband was a bright, handsome, and famously thoughtful man; so her choice must have surely been far from just venal. Whatever the case, in marriage she followed her mother, who'd married a WASP herself, moved closer to the metropolis, converted to Episcopalianism, and baptized her three children into that elastic denomination.

At all events, I'd have no grounds whatsoever on which to stake a proletarian claim. So it's curious, even to me, that from earliest memory I've chosen some of my most significant friendships from working class people. I'm not clear whether I've ever reflected at any length at least not on the page– on why this should be. It *has* been clear to me for ages that I find certain characteristics of the economic and/or intellectual elites abrasive, so that even in my life as an academic, using the term a bit loosely, I've largely avoided prolonged association with such folk with a couple of cherished exceptions, who know who they are.

I don't dismiss rags-to-riches or subliteracy-to-Ph.D. stories, of course, though in plain truth these are rarer than our sentimentalism insists, and are becoming more so in the opening decades of our century. In the majority of cases, whether or not financially rich, our elites inherited a good deal of social capital: at the very least, say, parents who were literate and decently educated. As for our alleged financial whizzes, many, perhaps most, inherited another sort of capital, as admittedly I did too, though whether I'm a leader I'll leave to others. It's not a theme that intrigues me.

What I'm getting at is an inexcusable inclination among elites of all stripes. Although, as the saying goes, the majority were born on third base, they seem to think they hit triples. If these fortunate sons (and in fewer cases daughters) fill the uppermost niches of American society, why, isn't that just the natural order of things?

I know a young woman in our part of Vermont whose background, to put it genteelly, is dysfunctional. She found herself pregnant quite early and soon fell into the lethal opioid epidemic that, as I write, enslaves so many. But she put herself into recovery, and went on to get her G.E.D. She's raising a toddler son now, all the while cleaning houses to meet expenses. She's also attending community college, holding a 4.0 GPA, with an eye to a B.A. in short order. Perhaps it's too easy to compare her lot, say, to Donald Trump's, but it doesn't take me any time at all to decide whom I regard as the more admirable.

The myth of upward mobility, then, is not *all* mythic. So-called American conservatives will point to prominent examples, avoiding evidence that these are increasingly uncommon. Though this is not a real Horatio Alger tale, since he did have significantly greater advantages, for example, than the woman I just lauded, I might point to my own great uncle. By the middle fifties, he had sufficiently enriched himself that he could lavish funds on his sister, my grandmother, in whose exurban Philadelphia house my parents also lived, and where they raised us five children. He was also generous to his niece, my mother, for whom he had served as a paternal surrogate, her own dad having died before she turned five. She deserved such reward, devoted and useful as she was to him from a very early age.

Uncle (as we tersely called him) was a daunting presence, and not only to me. He could be frighteningly judgmental, even volatile, and one longed to be elsewhere once his fuse got lit. He never had a romantic relation with any woman, and my siblings and I, picking up on some other clues as well, have since supposed him gay. Thus, given his historical epoch, private challenges may well explain much of that famous impatience and clamorous temper. It's a cliché of behavioral psychology, after all, that frustration engenders aggression.

Such Dancing as We Can

With his considerable wealth, Uncle bought a gentleman's property in the country. He was a skilled equestrian, and his high-bred horses were his heart's only darlings. But he owned beef and dairy cattle, too, along with hens and sheep. To manage these animals, and the crops that sustained them, he hired a certain Charles Grant. Mr. Grant and his wife Esther, Irish Protestant immigrants, had two children, Charlie, Jr. and Edmund.

Young Charlie was enough older than I that he figured primarily as an object of awe in my eyes, though not for long enough: at regular army basic training, very shortly after his marriage at nineteen, he died, absurdly, of the flu. This was 1955, my second year as a teenager, and that death introduced me to the concept of pure ruin. I recall how I, his idolater, felt an earthquake in my very soul, not to mention my pure wonder to behold his tough-as-nails, bull-necked father weep at the funeral, and the utter blankness on Esther's face, and the solemnity among contract workers, black and white, whom I'd always associated with hilarity and ribaldry (such as I understood it). All of this remains as stark in my mind as it was on the day that poor boy got buried.

But tragedy played no part in my feelings, on which a bit more directly, for his younger brother Edmund, or Eddie, who became my dearest friend from the first day I spent at what our family called, quite simply, The Farm. That is, from about the dawn of memory.

The Farm was my refuge for years, crucially important years at that. I had no way of properly knowing why I needed such sanctuary, as I suspect she didn't either, but family life was vexed in no small part by my mother's inchoate alcoholism. I can see this very clearly in hindsight, as in fairly short compass I became expert myself on the curse of addiction, though by the grace of God (and I mean that literally), unlike Mom I was blessed by recovery quite some time ago.

I harbored resentment toward my mother for too much of my life, and, to a lesser degree toward my sweet-tempered father simply for so often taking her part. Yes, he was an enabler, but he always treated me gently, and he died far too young at 55, a shock, needless to say, that rattled me far more than Charlie, Jr.'s sudden vanishing. It still does. But at length I recognized how unfair it was to curse anyone for sharing the same disease that afflicted me, the more so because that curse followed her to the grave. I could as fairly blame my father for the heart attack I had at 74, as if he had somehow willed his own on me, even if mine did not prove fatal like his. I couldn't change my mother when she lived. Why try after she died?

In the cases of both parents, rather than anger, I now feel sorrow about their fates. This is especially true of my mother, who had the longer, but undeniably the more painful life. As a young woman, she'd not only been beautiful but also endowed with sufficient academic ability to be admitted to the highly selective Radcliffe College. This accounts for part of my mother's attitude that especially galled me: her insistence that I never adequately applied myself at school. A-minuses were a disgrace, not to mention C-minuses (at best) for my performance in math, especially of the post-arithmetical kind, which no amount of application could remedy. I now recognize that, as the oldest of her children, I had become her academic vicar, and by her standards, less than valedictorian results amounted to crass squandering of opportunities from which she had been so unfairly barred.

Why such an assessment from her? Well, it seems that when she announced her Radcliffe news to her uncle, his response was concise– and surely devastating. "Women don't go to college."

Anyone who knew the old man would also know there'd be no appeal.

Again, perhaps, because she wanted me to redeem her frustrated intellectual aspirations, Mom felt disinclined, whether she knew it or not, to let me be a kid. Along with "Apply yourself," then, "Grow up" was a too familiar directive. The Farm was the place where my nose needed be to no grindstone. I could remain a boy, could ride my pony, camp in the woods, fish in the pond, plink cottontails with my minuscule .22, and indeed all of these, often enough, in the course of one outing.

And I could do everything along with Eddie, with whom I played Tonto and Lone Ranger, Cisco and Pancho, Batman and Robin, or any other commander-subordinate dyad we could imagine. We took turns being leader and sidekick, there being remarkably little competition between us, something unusual, for certain, among males of any age.

In short, until I got old enough to drive, which is to say to be intrigued by the opposite sex, and in fact for some years after, I spent every possible minute at Uncle's: winter and spring vacations, weekends, and those long, muggy, delicious summers. Eddie and I were inseparable companions there. My relations with Uncle reflected a mutual understanding: he was not a type to be much entertained by kids, and I was there not for him anyhow, but for the physical actuality of the Farm and for Eddie's company. My dealings with Uncle were therefore pretty much limited to peremptory morning and evening greetings. I was tolerated, or rather ignored, which suited me just fine.

So Eddie and I built hay forts and woods forts. We invented games, like the one in which we tried to land the flimsy boomerangs from the Johnson and Smith's novelty catalog in an outdoor watering trough. Once we got adept at doing so from one angle, we'd resort to a harder, and then a harder. Those were the cross-shaped boomerangs; when we graduated to the open V-shaped ones, we started to pretend that Esther's scarecrow, say, was a bad guy, and we'd try to take his hat off with our throws. Later, after Esther shooed us from the effigy in her truck garden, we tried to sneak up on woodchucks and cottontails, though all we ever did was scare them back into brush or burrow.

We were neither of an age to swap emotional secrets nor to philosophize. Indeed, if it had occurred to either of us to try, the other would likely have been mystified beyond response. It was what we *did* together that cemented our love; to this day, the way my heart leapt up on seeing Eddie after even a brief absence epitomizes what friendship can be. In some measure, that notion of common enterprise, whether it be shared enthusiasms as diverse as the reading or writing of poem or novel or (a touchy matter I'll glance at later along) the hunting of wild game– that sense of common enterprise is the basis of many a human bond to this day.

Not to hyperbolize nor fall into sentimentality, for us two this was an idyll– looking back on which, however, I sometimes marvel that we survived. We would smoke stolen cigarettes, for example, in our hayloft hideouts; having learned to drive the Farm's 1949 Army-surplus Jeep, we rolled it into a brook one evening without getting hurt; on another day, we took our axes to a sizeable maple, which fell upon us in a sudden gust of wind, the thick branches somehow coming down everywhere around us without touching either. In short, our adventures were ones that, had I known they involved my own kids (who doubtless had their perilous adventures too, however different the venues), would have frozen my blood.

But, as the famous epistle insists, there comes a time to put aside childish things. This meant acquiring some skills that were not designed merely to amuse or entertain.

Such Dancing as We Can

You could say that as poet and professor, I've more or less lived a life of the mind, but I have always considered it a misprision to assume that such a life is the only indicator of intelligence. If that were so, the nation's intellectuals would have non-functioning cars, toasters, faucets, airplanes —that list is infinitely protractible, of course— and they'd soon starve to death for want of food.

On which latter note, I can say from experience, even if or perhaps because my learning preceded the mechanized age of dairy— which now includes robotics!— that there's a right way to milk a cow by hand; indeed, try the wrong way and get no result. There is a proper technique to mowing and tedding hay, even to tying off burlap wheat sacks while the combine is moving full speed ahead. I suspect this may be why, in order to have value in my own eyes, whatever I may offer of so-called creative writing must be grounded in the palpable world.

I can reflect on these matters with some authority, however slight, because, as I reached early adolescence, I actually went to work summers on Uncle's farm, and on some others. Eddie was expected, nay required to do so by his parents. And what Eddie did, I did.

A local man named Roberts made a handsome living as a contract farmer; that is, he had the machinery and the crew for large-scale harvesting of crops. Landowners need not invest in expensive combines, bailers, what have you. Instead, they hired Mr. Roberts and crew as needed.

It may well be that this contractor hired me by way of staying on my uncle's good side; as a somewhat roly-poly and still quite short kid, I surely didn't make a very effective laborer. I couldn't pitch hay, for example, even like Eddie, two years my senior and quicker to mature. And of course I was *truly* feckless compared to seasoned adult co-workers. How painfully I recall struggling with heavy bales, chaff sticking to my neck in the dankness of mid-Atlantic summer, as I used every ounce of strength I had to heft my load onto a flatbed in motion. How red I must have turned when Willie, a migrant African-American laborer, a veritable Adonis, once chided me as he waited for a bale to reach him on the platform: "Boy, you'd ought to been born tall 'stead of fat."

Fact is, that labor was miserable in almost every respect, enough so that I check myself, as I would many a privileged professor, broker, or banker if I get to complaining about the work load I have to contend with. I do know what hard work feels like.

Yes, that farm labor was exhausting and meagerly remunerated, but if anyone had asked me, I'd have claimed to love it. I now see that this was, again, a matter of shared enterprise, one which, again like poetry itself for my money, has a definite *bodily* component. There's no doubt the field work toughened me up, and it showed me a whole dimension of life of which most of my suburban peers were entirely unaware. It inculcated in me a vivid appreciation of the physical fact, which, as Robert Frost somewhat mysteriously puts it in "Mowing," is "the sweetest dream that labor knows."

And speaking of the poet, I now believe early "literary" influences came upon me during our break times from field work, during which Mr. Roberts's crew (not the almost prudish man himself, who stayed clear), blacks, whites, Irish, whatever, would banter with one another. The conversation often had to do with the sexual appeal of women, though race track results and prospects, musical tastes, ball teams, automotive preferences, and so on figured in too.

I was struck not only by subject matter still more or less exotic to me (though, lying through my teeth, I sometimes let on otherwise) but also by the rich potpourri of idioms I sampled. One evening, for example, as we were finishing up an oat field, the neighbor's adolescent daughter, on whom I had one of my innumerable and impossible crushes, took a short cut across the fields to get to the paved road. The top was down on her dad's Ford, and her blond ponytail streamed in the breeze. Jim Campbell, a white man from somewhere in the south, commented that the sight was "enough to make a horse eat his own beddin'." I played at swagger, saying I'd like to ask that girl on a date. A normally laconic giant named Bill countered, "Like the man say, I axed for water and she give me gasoline." Everyone laughed, even the white laborers who, like me, probably didn't know this was a quotation from the great Delta bluesman Howlin' Wolf.

In short, what I came to see some time since is that nothing I write is other than a collaborative effort; what goes on the page inevitably carries the freight of myriad voices, and not just ones from the so-called canon or from academia but also from field and woods and alley.

One of the things that bonded me to Eddie was our shared enthusiasm for all that colorful palaver. We tried to import it into our own talk as often as possible. If we wanted to catch a grasshopper to fish for bass, we called it, like the so-called colored men we knew, a hopper-grass. I remember vividly walking out one morning to meet my friend: mist cloaked the pond, the farm animals were smudges out in the browning fields, and as we came together, we heard the single *tock!* of a woodpecker, a nostalgic sound for me to this day. "Peckerwood," we said in chorus, again echoing one of the black field hands from whom we'd heard it, though whether with reference to the bird or to a racist landlord, maybe, we could not have considered back then.

When asked where I am from, I often cite the name of the little town near The Farm. This is not quite a lie, in the sense that my uncle's spread became the home place of my imagination and in many ways persists as such, even if the neighborhood is no longer a pastorale but rather the domain of Staples, Domino's Pizza, Costco and the like. In those days for me, the area was simply *rife* with actuality and variety, unlike my all-white, well-fed hometown. I can get almost swoony now if I smell the interior of a cow barn, for example. The clamor of crows flocking to roost has a similar effect, as does fog lifting off water, or a certain timbre in a random black man's laughter. So on.

As I have made clear, I treasure an old cast of characters, in every sense of that term, some of whom played only cameo parts. I'll never forget the indescribable reek of someone banally named Paddy, goat-shouldered County Kildare farrier who'd show up in fall to re-shoe all the horses that had idled in pastures during weather too hot for riding. Nor will I forget his brogue-inflected whisper on encountering some setback: "Oh, for the want of the breath of life!" I still see his half-toothless, self-satisfied smile when, having plunged a perfectly fashioned shoe into a water pail, he stood from nailing it onto a hoof and pulled a little vial from his bib overalls. Before tipping it back, he'd whisper "Slainte" –whatever that meant; it didn't matter.

There was Normie, too, the slightly hunch-backed man of mystery who showed up in spring with a long, orange ferret in a burlap sack. The hens having all been shooed into an adjoining pen, he would release the ferret under their house. You could hear the scuffling and squealing until the predator had dispatched every rat and mouse he could find, whereupon Normie rang an oddly elegant silver bell, the ferret emerged, and back into the rough sack he went with seeming alacrity. The fetor of the tiny corpses under the house took a week or so to disperse.

If I were to continue this litany of recollection, I'd go on without stop. Come to think of it, maybe I have, at least for as long as I've viewed myself as a writer. I cited one poetic hero a paragraph or so, so how about another here? "The greatest poverty is not to live/ in a physical world," says Wallace Stevens.

Such Dancing as We Can

Amen, say I.

I had some other first-hand knowledge of a more colorful world via school, though not in the classroom. My small private day institution had a demerit system: accumulate four demerits for misbehavior and you were sentenced to grounds work come Saturday. One year, I showed up at Saturday detention for 36 consecutive weeks, missing just one, I think, in the academic calendar. When I –*I!–* was invited to give a talk to students at my 50th high school reunion (the only one I've ever attended), I noticed the august enfilade of lofty firs and spruces at the building's main entrance. Then it struck me: *I planted those trees!*

Or I helped a grown man to plant them. You see, I was a chronic weekend recidivist not merely because I couldn't control my impulses. True, I could not; but there was also the attraction of hanging out with Lovell, night- and weekend watchman and detention overseer. His collective name for the all-white student body was "cornfeds," but he called me "Stack o' Dollars." In turn, I called him "Money." We got on famously. I have encountered few with equal narrative gifts: his stories were simply *charged* with imagery and crackling dialogue. He could evoke the sights and sounds of a honkytonk club like no one I've ever heard since. His accounts of street fights were vivid and scary, his tales of romance both funny and stirring.

He was a bad-ass too, a rule-bender like me. Sometimes, when it was just us two, as it often seemed to be, we'd start a bonfire so that I could sit behind the smoke with him and share a cigarette or two, hidden from the respectable world.

Do you wonder that I racked up the demerits? Some of my friends, I suppose, were playing tennis at the local country club. I wouldn't trade places to this day.

Money also introduced me to a sort of music that had never been heard in my household or those of my friends. Crucial stuff. I mean not only vernacular music like that of the aforementioned Howlin' Wolf, or Bessie Smith or Jimmy Reed or Elmore James but also what multi-instrumentalist Roland Kirk called Black Classical Music, as exemplified in those days by late bop artists like Monk, Davis, Rollins, Gillespie, Roach and so on. Some have noted the penumbrae of this music in my own writing, and the plain fact is that this literary influence likewise came from a source that I feel blessed to have tapped. God bless you, Lovell, of cherished memory.

Money was a city slicker, so in the end he may have had less effect on me than men and women who were exactly his opposites. I remember them from boyhood too, especially after my parents bought an island camp in Washington County, Maine six decades ago. If any of these men and women still lived, they'd be well into their centenary years. They'd lived in this part of the world well before the advent of electricity and power tools. The men were saw- and axe-wielding lumberjacks or river drivers who floated log booms down the Machias River to the ocean every spring; the women –whom it would be laughable to label "housewives"– literally kept the home fires burning, and much more: they made clothing, dressed and preserved game and fish, did carpentry, tilled soil, split kindling, raised kids, and managed whatever else was necessary under harsh conditions.

If I say so, I have a lot of outdoor skills, a lot of savvy about woods and wildlife, how to hunt and fish, how to ply a canoe in whitewater, how to corn venison, how to drop a tree where I want it to fall, how to coax a flame from a wet log, how to cook over an open fire. On and on. These gifts were handed to me in great part by mentors like George and Creston MacArthur, Earl Bonness, Annie Fitch, Ada Chambers, and a dozen others.

But my professional debt to them is much akin to the one I owe that old scamp Money, because like him, they had extraordinary narrative talents (and in some cases, light-poetic ones too). Lacking any extrinsic entertainment, even from radio, they made their own, and, although many could scarcely read or write, their relish for the precisely eloquent detail and its perfectly apt rendering still motivates me. I loved the way their stories, in the manner of oral tradition worldwide, became community property. Even at 80, I continue to hear their voices every day –and I mean *every* day. Indeed, when I decided, quite late in life, to be a poet, my first collection not seeing print till I was almost forty, it was the rhythms and cadences of their language that I wanted to capture. I hoped the properties of poetry would allow as much without demanding imitation, because I knew myself insufficiently skilled to offer dialect without implying exactly what I did not feel for these beloveds: condescension.

When Earl's best friend Creston died, he looked out his shop window and into the dog-hair woods, full of waist-high snow: I'll never forget his expression as he said to me, "We made a lot of tracks together." How could he have framed so much of a world in such short compass? My heart brims with a treasury of equally compelling turns of phrase. If I have ever written a poem with that sort of gravity, in every sense of the term, then I am blessed, and I know the ones who blessed me.

Another crucial service these men and women rendered was likewise akin to one from Money Crawford, who would catch me up if I showed what he considered too lofty an opinion of myself. So did the Italian rogue Tony Calvano, who kept the building where I parked my motorcycle in grad school, and who always called me by both names at once. "Sydlea," he once asked, "just what happens in them classes of yours?" I did my best to describe a typical seminar, and he responded, more justly than he probably knew, "Sounds like bull crap in a three-piece suit to me."

Or how about Ernie Vauxhall, the African-American room inspector at Yale, who had stopped in while I sat at one of his and my favorite New Haven bars? The place was quiet but for us two and Ernie's pal, bartender Ike Dees, and, having forgotten my Friday duty call to my mother that afternoon, I asked if I could make a collect call from the bar itself. Ike assented, and when my mother answered, I claimed to be in the library doing research. At that point Ernie called out, "Hey, Ike, would you pass me the *Midsummer Night's Dream*?"

I assured Mom that that had been the voice of someone passing by in the Sterling Library corridor. Whether she bought it, I'll never know. I'd not likely have been able to explain that I was absorbing an important principle: to be too dead serious about oneself is to be alienated from what I can only and ineptly call things that matter.

That by happy accident I came into prolonged contact, from early on, with people whose financial and educational circumstances were so different from mine is, yes, a great blessing. I was about to say that as a result I've long known how to find cogent subject matter in unlikely places. In point of fact, however, if by now I truly thought them unlikely, it would mean I hadn't learned how misguided such a rubric is.

Indeed, the kinds of people I have been recalling turn out to be my *most* likely sources of "inspiration," to use a much-abused word, in my life. When Earl Bonness told me that he and his closest friend had made a lot of tracks together, he resorted to metaphor, but his figuration was grounded in a sensory world, just it was when he described a day as cold as a frog's mouth, or claimed that the night before had frozen an Inuit in his cellar. His remarks were not freighted with grandiose self-consciousness, and they were full of brotherly love.

Most of the members of my tribe, as Kathy Keizer called it, are at best uncomfortable with one crucial aspect of my connection to those old-time Yankees and their scions, namely that they and I are lifelong hunters. When I first came to the upper Connecticut Valley to teach, I was blessed almost immediately to befriend a number of the famously standoffish locals. The first friendship was with the road commissioner, Allie Pike, who noticed I kept a rabbit hound. Very soon we started to hunt snowshoe hares together. I taught the son of the local mechanic (himself another great raconteur) to hunt upland birds, and in due course became best man in his wedding. By the time I left that town, in order to stay above what my pal Tom Curren calls The Volvo Line, hunting had introduced me to just about every local family thereabouts, a matter that mystified other professors who'd moved there themselves.

And as I write, my dearest friend on earth is one of those locals; I've known him since his early boyhood too. (He is 14 years younger than I.) The man grew up, built our house, then broke our hearts more than a decade ago by moving to Colorado. He's among the smartest men I know, and hands-down the wittiest; but after a daylong jaunt in the woods with me, he confessed that he could barely read or write. He was in his late twenties then, and it was his admission that got me interested in adult literacy: soon after, I started as a tutor with Central Vermont Adult Basic Education, then joined its board for twenty years, for the last five of which I served as president.

Having outed himself, so to speak, my friend quickly corrected his problem, and has gone from being a hammer-swinger to a spectacularly successful contractor. We still get together for at least a week a year, and we stay in constant touch. I smile to myself each time I think, for example, of the clever nicknames he assigned to certain characters we both knew: "Woody Wide-Bite," say, for a fellow with hyper-conspicuous dentures, or "Freddy Folktale" for one who tended greatly to exaggerate and romanticize his achievements afield.

How did we come to be friends? We bonded as hunting partners in deer and grouse and duck habitat. He learned about bird dog training from me, as I had learned them from New England elders. Once more, I revert to the notion of shared enterprise in a physical world. I'll never explain to most salaried friends, let alone to PETA members, that the hunt for us is not simply a matter of slaughtering allegedly defenseless wildlife, but something sacramental. But I won't go farther here, having written two full books that largely deal with such an issue.

Such Dancing as We Can

One thing for sure: hunting wary game makes one conscious of how small a part one plays in the world's grand design. Which leads me at last to some concluding thoughts on why I shy away from "our tribe." The people I knew in my old town and their descendants– they are all gone now, as that part of the world turns into Fairfield County, Connecticut North. The new inhabitants believe they're living in the country, and to survey the surrounding landscape one might concur. Yet as my friend Dennis Covington recently wrote, "Geography is both in us and outside of us. No tracking device can substitute for the human heart." The heart of my old stomping grounds beats elsewhere now.

My instinctive predilection for working class companions has something to do with their straightforwardness. I don't mean to sentimentalize, because, like us all, the best of them have their character defects, some pretty distasteful. *But they're aware of what they're up to.* My aversion from the self-congratulatory "tribe" involves what I regard as their un-awareness.

Back to those farmers' markets. Like many of their patrons, my wife and I do all we can to stick with organic food; but I hope we continue to remember that such fare is out of reach for at least half the people we pass driving home from the market itself. Having woven their skirts of wool from the alpaca they bought with inherited mone, for $8000, or having hewn the wood –as natives have done for generations without expecting applause– that heated the sap for their maple syrup, too many tribespeople seem smugly assured that they model how to live now.

From time to time, my wife and I venture five towns south to an upscale grocery store, where we are often frustrated by two shoppers who meet in an aisle and simply block anyone from passing for as long as they share gossip. Many of these well-heeled consumers have signs in their yard saying, for instance, "I Love My Muslim Neighbor," but how often they ignore the fact that other neighbors are being inconvenienced by their self-absorption, not to mention the harried stock boys and girls, who might as well live on another planet for all the conversationalists appear to care.

Of course, I am being unduly judgmental and am scandalously over-general, but there it is. Such lack of consideration is borne, I believe, of a sort of *abstraction,* which is the quality of dealing with ideas as opposed to events. It derives, etymologically and aptly, from the Latin for *drawing away.*

Such Dancing as We Can

Drawn away from actuality, one too easily imagines that the world of his or her private construal is the only world that exists. In certain odd ways, my shoppers resemble many professorial types I've known, but also, to be fair, many poets. They spend so much time in one another's company–all the while preaching "diversity"– that they come to think their special concerns reflect the concerns of a broader society. Many are what Teddy Roosevelt described as "parlor radicals," elitists who preach anti-elitism, and who, in the presence of those they claim to champion, are as awkward as illiterates in a bookstore. I've witnessed as much over and over again. In their relentless effort to come up with new insights, they fly at such an altitude that the proverbial common man and woman can't even see them. They'd have been well served to know Tony Calvano as I did, the one, you may remember, who said my Yale seminars sounded like "bull crap in a three-piece suit." The clothes may have changed, but some things endure, especially at our so-called great institutions of learning.

That so many of my fellow self-styled progressives *do* fly at an exaggerated height suggests a lot about the coming into being of the lurid and fraught Trump phenomenon and his legacy– which, God willing, we may survive.

But that is surely stuff of a much, much longer story.

Sydney Lea

Such Dancing as We Can

REMORSE

When I noticed he'd brought along his damned accordion and had gone to his knees in what looked like prayer to open the case, I nearly shouted, *No!*

Have you ever recalled some minor misdemeanor of yours or even, as in this case, the thought of one, and felt that it caused disaster? Though what I describe is forty years old,

I remember strangling that scream and I still feel bone-chilling guilt. Absurd? Perhaps. But there it always is.

The man's tastes transcended old accordion chestnuts like "Lady of Spain." In fact, no matter your attitude toward the instrument, you'd have conceded his virtuosity: I'd heard him play Brahms, say, and then jump from there right into soul tunes from Stax, although the Stax, I don't have to add, went straight to the morgue on that box.

"Mustang Sally"? I ask you...

But I kept silent, thank God.

The dish my wife prepared was simmering in a big pot. For sociability's sake, she'd chosen one that needed no tending. But as soon as the guy slipped his arms through the accordion's straps, she sneaked away to the kitchen.

For my part, I grabbed a poker like a whodunit murder weapon and shifted some logs around in the fire– which likewise needed no tending. I loudly *oohed* about the embers' colors, as I'm sure he supposed we'd all be doing after we heard his performance, which lay in the offing.

The awful offing.

I resented, say, that he'd interrupt a conversation I was enjoying with a dear old friend about old whitewater paddle trips we'd shared. Before touching his keyboard, our accordionist looked at us and said, "I'm planning a river trip myself."

Back turned, I rolled my eyes and quelled a laugh. *That* guy on quick water? He was city, through and through.

Neither kitchen nor hearth would provide true escape, so I tried my best to conjure

some distracting daydream. *The offing, the offing.* I whispered the words twice over.

Maritime words.

As he started "Smoke Gets in Your Eyes," I closed my own eyes. Perhaps he'd think

Such Dancing as We Can

I'd been carried away– which I had, but not, as he may have imagined, by his performance.

Rather, I'd summoned the soughing of surf, the scent of salt air, damp sand that squealed as I walked, and sails far out– *in the offing.*

I saw stranded horseshoe crabs, wrack washed up from the bay, gulls as ever squabbling over this or that bit of decay. I almost smelled death's pungent, primal odor.

Then quick as that, the music died.

Back then I rejoiced. Today I shudder. Yes, it *is* absurd to assume responsibility for driving that musician onto white water in June of that very same year. He went of his own accord and lost his life. Had he really played "Drown in My Own Tears" that night? No, this must be my guilt talking again.

My love brought out the pot and lifted its lid to applause, which I'd bet the accordionist thought was meant for him. He should have known better. How could he imagine he'd master rapids in an open canoe? He couldn't have told you the difference between a J-stroke and a breast-stroke. I probably should have said something.

But I guess I figured what a fool doesn't know can't hurt him.

Such Dancing as We Can

ALL THINGS BRIGHT AND BEAUTIFUL

> He gave us eyes to see them
> And lips that we might tell
> How great is the Almighty
> Who has made all things well
> *—Cecil Frances Alexander*

On this icy morning, the notion of staying in bed greatly tempted me, engrossed as I was in a book of John Singer Sargent's watercolors, not to mention in the pleasure of warmth under the comforter. But when the sun crept over the hills, our dogs began their usual whoofing and baying downstairs. They needed to get outdoors to empty themselves and to romp in the snow.

So there I stood, a little daunted on the first of December, in a northwesterly blow, beholding that too-early snowfall. I steered the dogs away from our pond, whose ice won't yet quite hold them.

It does support other weights: the prints of a pigeon-toed porcupine had scrawled themselves across the surface, and for no good reason save for the recent exposure, I thought of Sargent's crucified Christ, how His feet alone convey the scene's brutal pain. I felt an instant of compassion for the porcupine, forced now to search even more strenuously for sustenance amid these new exigencies of weather.

Then I thought of that animal's cassock of spikes, from which he'd readily have spared some scads for our dogs. I rehearsed two endless waits and exorbitant expenses at the emergency veterinary clinic this past summer and that minor compassion evaporated. We can't be sure the villain was the same one that keeps mauling the boards on our backyard porch, but our animosity is the same. We've often fooled porcupines with baits of melon or bark steeped in saltwater, but this one's cagey: it has shunned our live trap since September.

As I shivered, I visualized another Sargent: "Mountain Stream," which depicts a placid summer's day. Just then I longed for such calm, the cold and the tracks having moved me to rage, my mind apparently bound to go wherever it wanted. Even in this frigid lull, I briefly relived my hot reaction to a *neighbor's* rage. The man flew a flag a couple years back with the slogan *Fuck Joe Biden*. Whenever we passed, we always prayed for wind to be still, for that inexcusable inscription to be hidden in the slack. This had mercifully been the case each time we had our six-year-old grandson with us, because he'd have quickly decoded that sentence.

Without any smugness or affectation, the child is precocious, so he might even, however vaguely, have sensed the meaning of words from an old-time Sargent critic: "His every touch was individual and conveyed a quick unerring message from the brain... a kind of shorthand, but magical." I'm not sure why this remark still lingers in my head this morning. Something about hasty messages, perhaps.

Our neighbor's family has lived in our tiny town since before it was founded. There's an NRA sticker on his beater pickup truck. I loathe that NRA crowd and all it stands for, but I do own hunting arms, and I admit I've frequently considered murder– of the porcupine, I mean.

To see those freshly gnawed boards on our porch makes me so angry I've considered ripping one up and using it for bait. Maybe *that* would fool him. I'd take our loathsome invader to an unclaimed, rotting lumber pile down by the river. Let him gnaw there all he wants!

I try to govern my rancor, but fellow feeling involves work when it comes to an animal. As for that bile-spewing neighbor of ours, it's a genuine labor, though I was taught as a child to revile the sin and forgive the sinner.

There's a lot of wisdom in that caution: if I indulge my fury, I tread on thin moral ice. Maybe we all do when it comes to tolerance. One shouldn't detest something or someone merely for being what it is.

Still, I confess I'd gladly learn that our nuisance was a corpse.

Such Dancing as We Can

BLUES
    --May 2020

Another unarmed black man has been gunned down by police. Great cities erupt, but the *thin blue line*– what else?– is established to contain that predictable response.

Meanwhile, as daylight dies here in Vermont, I catnap on my couch, remote from mayhem and fury, retired, financially secure, ashamed of my own comfort.

Half-conscious, I watch my mind stray from metaphoric to identifiable blue, like the wetland iris I beheld on this morning's hike; like the blue sulfur butterflies, hovering close to ground, arrived again with spring; like the luminous indigo bunting last week at our feeder, a miracle.

"Blue Monday" was recorded long ago by the late Fats Domino. I loved that tune in his rendition, and to think of it now, prompted by a mere adjective, is to lament the thrust of time. Of course. Yet I've largely been spared more epical sorrows.

My bourgeois woes are as common and small as many of the things I notice. This May, for further instance, the wild violets are rampant. Little things like that. Soon, the darkness will shroud the landscape and some creatures will search for refuge, while others prepare to wreak their violence. No, that expression doesn't ring quite true. What they'll do is what predators must do in the natural world.

On the far side of the ridge, there's a wailing train, a sound that has prompted music of a kind I dearly love. You know what kind I mean, though it's not restricted to the ingenious likes of Hank Williams, white Alabaman, who by the way got his first guitar lessons from black bluesman Rufus "Tee Tot" Payne. No, the blue in that sound is part of every stirring vernacular music America has ever engendered.

But of course there are larger blues. The sky, for the most obvious example. As its color recedes, I remember a grandchild clad entirely in blue for Halloween last fall. She wanted to be the sky. From her father she gets the African blood for which I pray to whatever God I can invoke that she and her brother and sister won't have to suffer. I shudder.

I try to will myself back into trance, but I can't. I want to dream up a blue that forever assuages, a blue in which I could paint the world.

Such Dancing as We Can

Who in hell do I think I am? Whom do I help with my poetical fancies?

Through a screen, I hear night creatures begin to hoot and shriek. The dark is taking over.

Sydney Lea

Anosmia

One of my two younger sisters and her wife contracted COVID-19 late in 2020. That sister's sense of smell has not returned since.

I was about to say I'd never much thought about such an ailment, but come to think, I had briefly pondered it a decade before, when I was still a college teacher. I recall prompting a student to tell me a back-story during office hours, because her written story for class discussion contained a word that the narrative never defined. It mentioned, more or less in passing, that her protagonist had anosmia. Then it went on pretty conventionally about how the girl, who came from a NASCAR family, once fell for a certain race driver, apparently somewhat famous. Predictably, the affair ended in heartbreak.

I had no interest in automobile racing, and, even if I had, the love plot would have been too familiar: exactly the kind of thing, I'm afraid, I'd read by many aspirant young authors of all genders. I knew that the account represented real urgency on this one's part, but it just couldn't hold an older reader like me. That sort of jadedness was a key factor in moving me to retirement shortly after. I didn't want to feel even a jot of contempt for young people merely because they were young. I too clearly remembered being on the other side of such disdain.

Anosmia, though— well, I'm a sucker for out-of-the-way words, and I wanted to own this one. It appears that her dad was an EMT, and as a child she peeked inside his satchel one evening. She asked about the smelling salts. When her father explained their use, she begged him for a whiff. Though he didn't want to, he gave in, partly because it was the girl's ninth birthday. She sniffed the open vial, and that marked the last moment in her life when she could smell. Anosmia is the clinical term for such loss.

Yes, I did find that a better and sadder tale than what she'd submitted. I was intrigued, thinking that in my own case and perhaps most people's, the capacity to experience odors is essential to feelings of nostalgia or joy or revulsion—the list goes on.

Smell is also closely linked with the sense of taste, and I asked my student about that. She said that the only food she cared for at all had to be highly spiced: certain Thai or Mexican or Indian dishes. Her mom had quickly been obliged to introduce such fare to her balky midwestern family.

164

Sydney Lea

It happened that she recounted all this on yet another birthday, her 22nd. I offered her best wishes as she left my office. By my reckoning I was not all that much older than her father, and I thought hard about his cursed luck. The man had repressed his reservations so he could oblige a child on her birthday. What followed must have devastated him.

Driving home, I looked through my windshield at a hard-edged January moon, and beside it, Aldebaran, the brightest star in Taurus. Now if unlike me you have faith in that sort of thing, you believe people born under the sign of the Bull are pushovers for sensuous gratification: wet kisses, good wine, rich food, so on. But mysticism aside, I wondered how it can possibly feel to have made a small mistake that so altered the life of your child? You must keep replaying that moment, wishing it could be undone.

And then, again because my mind –or perhaps anyone's—rarely follows an orderly sequence, I thought of Dick, the old Vermont lumberjack I'd known when I was slightly older than that young woman. He married twice, his first wife having died in birthing their fifth child, who died during delivery too. He fathered two

Such Dancing as We Can

more children with his second spouse, who outlived him by almost twenty years.

Dick's manner was terse, and he had a nose for bald truth. I suddenly recalled something he said, and not only about working in the woods: There's always a trap set for you.

When I got out of my car at home, I gazed up at the moon again. It looked as sharp as one of Dick's axes.

Sydney Lea

STORYTELLING AT THE RES

Joe hopes he's a good guy now, but by jollies he wasn't a good one once. He says he even stole his own wife's hairlong jewelry to pay off a deal.

I have to smile: *hairlong*.

If you need a drink or drug, Joe continues, believe me, you'll take what you got to take. Go ahead and rob your buddies or, like he just said, even your very own folks.

Outside, cold rain is coming steadily, but it feels so warm indoors I'm afraid I'll doze, even though I'm not exactly sleepy, and Joe's story isn't boring. Not at all.

There was a time he worked a big saw, he says, and the whole while plastered. It's a wonder he never got himself or somebody wasted. There was a lot of days like that, and a lot in the joint too. Once he broke a white cop's arm with a tire iron. The cop and his pals didn't like that, you can bet.

Joe wears a raven feather in his hat, which he jokes about, telling how it shows he's gotten better, because it sure isn't no war bonnet. He tries to stay humble is what he's saying, just that one feather. He prays all his war days are done for.

Anybody else got something? he asks now. Everyone nods, but afterwards most just look shy and keep their mouths shut, except one guy in the room whose tribal name is See-Quickly, but people call him Jesse. He wears braids and has half an arm missing. He speaks up just enough to say he's glad he's out of prison. Again. I hear some scattered applause.

They's a bunch of other people *not* here, Joe says, some of them clean and sober for years. Then they disappear, and then you hear they're locked up, or else dead.

What about you? Joe asks, looking at me, one of the few white guys. What you got?

I try to say something, but it seems too hard to come up with anything except I'm happy to be here, which I guess is true.

No, no, don't nobody feel on the spot, Joe continues, shaking his head, which makes his jowls shake too. He's just a guy himself with some habits. Like check out this gut– too many doughnuts.

Sydney Lea

But doughnuts don't make you lose it. I want to say that, because we are all in this place for being crazy once.

You got something more, Jesse? Joe asks. Let's hear about it. Once you put stuff right out in the open, see, that helps you get it out of your system. You start in with that, then maybe you can get some healing.

Jesse says, I don't even own no hat, never mind some bonnet. I ain't got shit.

Joe calls that God's will for now.

So when I chopped off my arm at the mill, that was God working his ways on the res? Jesse asks Joe, but he isn't pissed off; or anyhow he smiles.

Joe knows Jesse didn't mean anything bad. What happens, whatever it is, is what happens, he says. You might as well think there's a reason for it. I mean, check around here. Joe nods his head at everyone in his seat. I look down at the floor when his eyes get to me. We're supposed to be where we're at. I just call that a God deal, even when our asses get throwed in stir, maybe even if we're killed. What do I know? I don't know what God is, except He ain't me.

Such Dancing as We Can

I wonder if what he says next might not just be right, and it could include me: we all went to different schools together.

My trouble is, I want a story, and not just any story, but a knockout like Jesse's. The fact that I keep looking for that sort of thing means maybe I'm not so much better than I was when I was using after all. I have to be a lunatic or just a fool to have wishes like that, to believe I haven't been beat up enough to be interesting.

The blue tattoo on Jesse's stub shows only the top halves of letters; I can't make out the word they spell.

Sydney Lea

STICKING TO FACTS

As I lay in bed, I vowed to record the dream's details: the mocha river, the wooden dock, the boy, and the older man, who may have stood for me, though I hope not. Those specifics alone seemed so cogent that I kept urging my half-conscious body to get up and write them down, believing they boded revelation. But to leave my bed– its pillow so soft, its blanket so kindly– proved beyond me.

No matter, as it turned out. I retained the physical data and more. I clearly pictured the elderly man as he leaned over a rail, advising the boy that the river's anger meant a hurricane coming. This sounded exactly backward to me, but something about the speaker's response to objective things implied that his knowledge, while focused on material laws, pointed at realms beyond it.

The boy, all overalls, freckles, and cowlick, might have played a role in some bogus, sentimental movie about farm life. For all his bumpkin appearance, however, his nature seemed an inquiring one, and he clearly trusted in his senior's wisdom.

But what the old man suggested next was dismayingly banal. He said that the dock below could be ripped from

Such Dancing as We Can

its posts by storm. "Hence the chain," he added, meaning one that ran from the dock itself around an oak. "It will hold everything together," he vowed, and yes, he used that archaic *hence,* as if such elevated diction could elevate his drab commentary too.

Soon the hurricane roared in. Its wind all but instantly snapped the chain and spun the dock downstream. The old man ginned up new explanations for these developments. He claimed, improbably and incomprehensibly, that in fact all this tumult validated his haphazard inklings.

The minute I came awake, I recognized the old man's talk for the rubbish it was. As so often in my experience, especially as a writer, what had seemed so promising in sleep turned out to be drivel by the light of day.

Having braced my wits with caffeine, I went down to the village post office, where I ran into our townsman Will. He's been on my mind since we loitered outside, chatting about this and that. I can't help marveling at how he confronts the physical aspects of *his* life. Working on a roof a few years ago, he fell from a ladder. Seven operations have ensued– all useless. He has to wear a monstrous boot. Even standing is painful, never mind walking.

Sydney Lea

I mean anything but condescension when I say it's unlikely Will much considers dreams, rubbish or otherwise.

He told me he'd gotten a cashier's job at a diner, where he could stay seated for most of the day. His boss provided him with a tall stool; he said that boss was a good person and he liked him; he even claimed to enjoy the new position. In short, Will appeared upbeat, but then he always does.

If I made Will into a hero, I know he'd roundly resist. Still, I can't help admiring his pragmatism and valor. Right after the last procedure went wrong, he told me, *Bad things can happen to people, so why not me? I fell off a ladder, that's all.*

Typical unadorned language, unadorned fact– to which Will always sticks. He's utterly unlike the old man in my dream, handing the boy his mystical bunkum even after the chain let go and the dock went hurtling seaward.

I trust I don't engage in such hogwash myself. But I've been a poet a long, long time, so I can't be sure.

Such Dancing as We Can

EVERYWHERE

Everywhere *what?* You thought I'd be saying violence. I will, but I'll say more.

There's been ruthless war somewhere since I can remember but here on a cold February day there's our younger son's voice as he calms *his* younger son just after the kid has skinned his knee while learning to ride on two wheels.

Stop right where you are. I know: skinned knees and weaponized rape or torture– well, it's lightning bug and lightning, as Mark Twain so famously said. And yet.

My brother is forty years dead today. As I've mentioned, it's a familiar old grief. I rekindle it on skimming the poet Novalis, of all the cock-eyed, moony romantics, as he prattles in "Hymns to the Night":

> *Your luster must vanish*
> *Yon mound underneath–*
> *Cool shadows will bring thee*
> *Thy wreath.*

I don't know if that's meant to reassure or not. It does neither for me, maybe only because I don't have any idea what's meant here. So why am I wiping my eyes and nose with my sleeve? How many sleeves would I need if that

Sydney Lea

knee-skinned little boy or his brother or some of his first-cousin friends had been one of the multiple child deaths in the Ukraine or one of the murders in my gun-clutching Land of the Free, Home of the Brave?

Violence-violence-violence. My pains and joys are plain vanilla, compared. Okay. But that doesn't make them vanish. So why not call on that moon-bat Novalis again?

> *I feel the flow*
> *Of Death's youth-giving flood*
> *To balsam and ether*
> *Transform my blood.*

Get lost, I say. And that's what he did. At 29.

And here I am, surrounded by ample blessings. I tell myself, *Count them,* and often I do,

like that little knee-skinned boy and his brother and his good father and mother, his father's and mother's brothers and sisters, those five precious cousins I spoke of before.

Okay, call me the Merchant of Treacle. Sticks and stones.

And look: I do keep moving. I'm still not overwhelmed. No, I'm not –at least not yet– overwhelmed.

Such Dancing as We Can

TEMPORARY BACHELOR

A sorry time to recollect. Perversely enough, it would shortly make the COVID lock-down feel like a relative blessing– for me, I mean– because my wife was with me for almost every minute of that isolation. Sometimes my self-serving is indefensible.

This morning, she is simply out on a long, solitary walk in the woods, the sort she often takes, but even her temporary absence brings to mind a longer one two years back when she went on a trip with her younger sister.

Though unhungry, I cracked a single egg one morning, a trifling matter that lingers in mind for no especial reason. Had she not been away, the two of us would as ever have applauded its yolk's deep orange, scoffing at the pallor of store-bought. In the prior week, I'd noted color of any kind only vaguely. Had she been here, we'd have praised our village bank branch's cheery manager for raising free-range hens and selling those bold-yolked eggs the from the bank itself.

Our one train groaned down the valley. Eight hours later it would come back up as ever. It makes that round trip every day.

Sydney Lea

How on earth do widowers get by? I should always dwell on my good luck, keep my transitory woes in proportion.

There's a certain way my wife can cock her hip that stirs me. So does the familiar, bracing scent of her skin when she comes in from cold like today's. I am eager to know it again when she gets back from her walk. But she didn't come in on the day I recall, and one luminous egg was not nearly as eloquent as that single plate I brought to the sink.

I smile now in spite of everything, noting that in my retirement and my rare solitude, self-indulgence meant leaving the toilet seat up. *La vida loca,* all right!

After breakfast, I planted myself in the kitchen rocker to wait until her noontime call, two old dogs curled at my feet. The day gaped, like all before. Waiting there, I remembered a hike we took together in the lesser Dolomites, part of our honeymoon forty years back. Far below, a tarn winked like a diamond. And later, no dish of fettucine ever tasted better than the one we shared in that *paese* at the mountain's base.

Come afternoon, I'd briefly distract myself by discharging small chores: feeding the same old chickadees and pine

Such Dancing as We Can

siskins, checking the woodstove far more than was needed, re-washing that plate, though it wasn't really dirty. She'd be gone another full week, I calculated. I tried to bless both sisters.

When we were young, my wife's *r*s were childlike. I loved that, a thing I'd forgotten about until just then, when I suddenly missed the inflection. I used to make her recite phrases that brought *r*s to the fore, "veterinary clinic" a favorite. I've come to regret that my amusement moved her to alter her diction.

From my chair, I beheld the hillside out the kitchen window, with its marvelous network of shadows laid onto the snow by a radiant late-winter sun through the trees. Hardwood buds grew red on the ridges. They do that each year of course.

I remember putting my elbows on the table, hands to my temples, grateful that I was the only one to witness my weeping.

Sydney Lea

Army Specialized Depot #829, 1942

I take down a formal photo of my father, seated 81 years ago with his "colored" troops, backgrounded by a grim-looking fort in Alabama. For the Yankee company commander of people whom townsfolk– if they wanted to sound broad-minded– referred to as *nigras,* the place was a threatening one, especially because he now and then had groups of his soldiers in for meals or drinks. That made for local fury and, once, for a cross burned outside his bungalow. Of course, those soldiers of his had faced far greater perils– and they'd face more when they got overseas.

But back to the picture: Dad's there with eighty troops and two other white officers. "We were a busted flush," he joked. I hardly need add that I never knew those men, but these ages later, as I contemplate their expressions, each at least outwardly stoic, I feel some odd combination of flame and lead in my guts. Is there anyone left to remember the person to whom each face in the photograph attests?

Their lives amounted to unfairness and often enough pure terror. Then anonymity. Doesn't human vileness sometimes move you to think that our species' elimination might truly be something to hope for?

There I go, as bloated with righteous indignation as any adolescent, addicted to simplification, intent on black and white. But for the love of God, there *are* certain unforgivable evils. Agreed?

Perhaps not. Consensus these days seems almost quaint.

I write in a different world, though not entirely different, alas. Here, a midwinter gale commands each tree to salaam. After the war, I would come to know my father's gentle command. I can replicate the sound of his laughter in mind, how he'd soothe me after some minor injury or insult, the way he'd whistle when he walked through the door from work.

What sort of work? Who knew? Who cared? He made waffles on Sunday. He hugged me. He sang, "Three Times Round Went Our Gallant, Gallant Ship." I won't forget all that and much, much more.

Outside, dark gathering, Dad's image seems almost to blend with his soldiers' in the photograph. Then they all disappear. My mother is long dead too. I have younger brothers and sisters, none truly young any longer, of course. Does any of them, like me, recall the very scent of this good man's sweat, or am I the last?

Such Dancing as We Can

NAKED TREES
--for Goran

Small Hercules in a small Augean Stable, I've been trying to tidy my writing room. And yet what I'd imagined would be a quotidian chore is in fact teeming with surprises.

One especially: it's an ambered snapshot that has lain for years in a piece of mail from back when we all used mail. The photograph shows a man outside a Serbian prison's wall. Under the crude, uncomposed image there's a scrawl in rough English that I can barely decode: *My hotel twenty months.*

The picture is old now. In it, my friend the poet is a younger man smiling. Yes, however indistinct his face, he's impossibly smiling.

That letter and its contents got buried somehow until just now, so I've never asked him who held the camera. I *will* ask if, please God, we're blessed to see each other again– and if I remember. The older I am, the more things slip my mind. Travel's gotten daunting too. I'm tired, he's far away.

Sydney Lea

Despite that smile, there's much *he'll* never forget, like his brother done in by a sniper, among countless other horrors of which he never speaks in any detail.

A monument stands in the square by the jail, perhaps a tribute to some singer or painter or actor once hailed and now forgotten; or to a battlefield triumph, also forgotten; or maybe to a workers' paradise, unachieved.

There are snowed-over café tables in the background of the statue and prison. I can just make them out through an enfilade of plane trees whose foliage has been blown off by shelling.

The naked trees chill me. I may never see my friend again.

Of course, such a concern is nothing compared to his memories of pain and grief. I suspect my despair is amplified by how flawless an emblem those plane trees are of a general human devastation.

Such Dancing as We Can

BRIGHTER FOR ABSENCE

I passed the site of the old Colby Block last week. I never gave that stretch of real estate too much thought until I watched it burn. Its buildings sprawled along the west shore of the Connecticut River, its northmost one a food market. To the south stood a little house where a video store did a healthy business. In those days, such places existed. I remember renting *The Sword and the Stone* there, and our son watching it dozens of times in his fifth year. Children, counter to adult mythology, prefer iteration to novelty. At my age, I do too.

The video store survived the fire. Its owner was a great big blond guy, whom people who knew him called Truck. I called him by his given name, Calvin, just to stay safe. Others, even ones who didn't really know him at all, claimed he peddled drugs as well as movies. I had no grounds for judgment either way.

Our family moved upriver over thirty years back. By then, Truck had sold out to a fireworks business. Or maybe he'd already sold out and the next owner passed the building on to the fireworks place. I'm hazy on the details, but they don't much matter.

I heard Truck died shortly after we left that neighborhood. Sad. He was still more or less young.

The eponymous Mr. Colby ran a shop in the complex, as his father had before him. It dealt in obsolete clothing, not that that was the proprietor's intention– no retro-hip for his establishment. It was empty when fire took it. He had shut the place down and retired well before the disaster He died perhaps a decade ago, but as an old man, unlike Truck.

Happily, we soon heard that no one got hurt in the conflagration. As for the buildings, the fire department had little choice but to stand by, guarding the rest of the neighborhood from the inferno that reduced so much to cinders in a few hours. I found myself among the rubberneckers across the road. I'd been passing through town and noticed the tank trucks and the crowd.

One remembers strange details. At one point, I looked away from the devastation and down route 5. I watched a cat– old fighter, I judged, tatterdemalion, missing an ear– as he crept toward a bush. To him, it must have been just another evening.

The bush was a double-flowering plum, or so I'd been told by a local nurserywoman. I kept meaning to buy one and plant it at our house down that way, but never got around to the job. And then we moved. I *have* planted one here, but it doesn't seem to flower as splendidly as the plum I beheld that night, which still blooms bright and pink come May.

This was middle August anyhow. There weren't any flowers. The tom made a rush, flushed a sparrow, and missed it. Now there, now gone.

Nobody has built on the block since that night long ago. Nowadays I rarely pass where everything stood, but when I do, it's as though I look through the buildings' ghosts to the quaint New Hampshire town just across the river. To me, those fancied old structures resemble photographic negatives. That was our town on the other side back then, though we lived deep in the woods beyond it.

Yes, I largely ignored the block until I saw it burn. Now when I do go by, I pay it more attention.

Once we lived even farther away, ten miles south, in yet another village, where Landers, an impoverished bachelor townsman, burned to death in his shack one Fourth of July. He'd kicked a kerosene lamp in his sleep. Now there, now gone.

I'm not sure why Landers occurs to me now, but for the thought of fire– and that he shines brighter now for his absence, just like those charred stores, or Truck, or Mr. Colby the haberdasher.

Such Dancing as We Can

ONE MORE EULOGY
–in mem. Forrest Bartlett (1936-2011)

I'd arrived a bit late, and the lot at the church had filled up. So I parked in a spot by the shady lawyer's office, which was closed on a weekend afternoon.

By the time I ran in, the tributes had already started, rough and funny and tender all at once, just like the dead man himself. We heard words I suspect had never been heard in that sanctuary, and wouldn't be heard again, but without them, none of us —over two hundred strong– would have found the hour right and true.

Our old friend was a jack-of-all-trades. He logged, he farmed, he did bodywork on cars, and whenever he could, he went hunting. The reminiscences tended to dwell on all that. *One of a dying breed:* the phrase kept repeating itself, as if it had been invented for him. Nowadays the breed's descendants have generally left the farm, but they haven't found a better thing to take its place. Most live in trailers or shabby apartments, and the only hunting they do is for work, which has lately been scarce.

Even if I hadn't watched some tough people cry that day, I'd have cried on my own, just as I'd have laughed even without hearing others' laughter, or the jokes told aloud by an arty-looking woman about how she, a Vegan, for the love of God, could have loved him so.

Sure, he could get worked up, said his friend John the blacksmith. *He might take a poke at you.* But John reminded us as well that he'd be there if you called him for help *with your cow or your wood or your heart.* The dead man didn't want preachers at his burial, so it was the blacksmith who spoke the eulogy, a word whose meaning, he admitted, he'd had to look up: "A formal speech in praise of someone who's died."

I wouldn't have called John's eulogy formal, merely perfect. Cow or wood or heart indeed. Furthermore, what it said was all true. Try making the same claim for that lawyer, for the politicians, for the smug professors.

John ended the service with "After Apple-Picking" by Robert Frost, partly because another of our late friend's callings was that of cider-maker. As I say, he did more or less whatever he could do to get by.

Where I'd parked was not, after all, the lot for the shady lawyer but for the tenants who lived above the next-door laundromat. A tattooed woman with a basket of wet clothing, her voice rough with smoke, got all worked up

Such Dancing as We Can

because I'd taken her space. *I don't give a shit why you're here,* she snarled. My temper might easily have flared; yet all I could find to say was, *I'm sorry. Jesus, I'm sorry.*

Sydney Lea

SUNDAY MORNING

A gorgeous day in May, leaves in pastel, serviceberry flowers conspicuous at our field's edge. Two warblers keep flitting in and out of view. A cardinal twitters from a basswood, which longs to burst into bloom as well. Amid these sensory pleasures, I think of that woman in "Sunday Morning," the most famous of Wallace Stevens's poems, who feels *complacencies of the peignoir,* perhaps on a morning like this.

For my near neighbor Dub, it's a working day at the abattoir. I'm not sure why his time off comes midweek. The gap between some lives and others can be confusing– and distressing, if we lucky ones ever ponder it.

There are those, I'm sure, who on picturing Dub will smother a yawn. I understand. He doesn't seem in any way exotic, nor of course does his lousy job. He leaves his trailer at 7:00 or so and spends all day in the slaughterhouse. Home after 5:30, he cracks a Bud, and that's about that, but for a quick bite and a sitcom perhaps, provided it airs early enough. Eight hours of doing what Dub does would tire anyone, or so I suspect.

Such Dancing as We Can

How, for example, might the permanent stains on his hands concern you? To be frank, I don't know. I don't know what I make of them myself. Dub and I are friendly, but we don't engage in much beyond small talk.

I do know that his left ring finger was hewn at the knuckle quite a few years ago. I can remember when he was secretive about that injury, keeping the disfigured hand in his pocket or behind his back as much as he could. Maybe he was afraid people would judge him badly for awkwardness or would simply find the stub unsightly. He appears well past such concerns by now. Still I try not to look at the maimed hand, much less ask about it. Did he cut the finger off with a saw? A knife? A machine? I have no idea.

I can imagine some artsy type —one with an attenuated version of Wallace Stevens's sensibility, perhaps— likening the flow of his blood that day to a meteor shower or some such fanciful thing, a worthless gesture, I'd insist, even a contemptible one. Come to think of it, I've always been slightly irked to read another passage in a Stevens poem:

At dawn,
The paratroopers fall and as they fall
They mow the lawn.

My guess is that those paratroopers might see the matter rather differently. But maybe we let Stevens get away with such writing, first, because he was a greatly gifted poet and, second, because he was insured.

Dub has a cousin here in the village. People who know him better than I do call him Croaky– just another working stiff who ekes out an existence as he can. He mows lawns, digs graves, sells bait, runs errands for old folks. He also fells and splits hardwood for the fireplaces of those who can afford to buy the logs rather than cut their own. A few teach at the local college, and many of them ask for white birch, though it isn't much for coals. They just like how it looks in the hearth before any flame takes hold, and how it crackles and snaps when the bark catches. Croaky calls it *Professorwood*.

The poor guy pulverized a shinbone in 2000. Does this sort of mishap run in the family? It's said he was swinging his maul when a toad hopped out of the brush and caught his attention. The hammer glanced off the block and slammed his leg. That's when people who know him a lot better than I do pinned the nickname on him. His name and his limp are the wages, some may assume, of being feral, crude, and careless. I call him Ron.

Such Dancing as We Can

Dub's stump, Croaky's halting walk— how should we treat such matters? Not at all, perhaps. Better to warm ourselves by our fires, complacent, dreaming of tropics, or high art, or refreshing morning dew. So much is there for us after all. We only need a little leisure to appreciate it.

Mind you, I say *we*. I have no right to sanctimony.

Sydney Lea

NOVEMBER, 1981

I was gripped by a real sorrow: my young brother had just died of a brain aneurysm. He was only 35.

Of course, no one ever anticipates that sort of crisis. What does one do? What *can* one? As for me, I unaccountably set out into a wildness called Breaux's Gore, a place I'd never been, and one where –in the proverbial middle of nowhere– I came on a headstone, knife-thin, canted.

The morning was quiet. Never such quiet. Was there anyone who knew that marker beside me? Even now who knows about it? The odd hunter, I suppose. The slab has been there since 1841, in open country at the start, country that had reverted to doghair-dense woods. I read the name on the marker: *John Goodridge*, a man perhaps wife- and childless. Weather had worn the headstone's shoulders round.

I hiked out to my truck and drove home. As evening approached, I moved back and forth from woodpile to shed. The process felt less like work than dream. Odors rose on November's twilight, then settled. Sawdust, rain, the logs I'd split the week before. I settled too, sitting in our wheelbarrow's bed, my seeming self like a chunk of maple or dirt or stone that might ride along in muteness.

It's been more than four decades since I found that marker, the same since my brother trod God's green earth; but how specifically I recall the way all the world went silent near that grave. That was a silence more entire than any I've ever known before or since.

I will never forget it. I will never be able not to hear that utter absence again. Darkness was coming now, the days having shortened so. From the wheelbarrow, I looked around me.

Our young family was all set for the real coming cold; I could almost hear the subtle hum of our old Round Oak woodstove.

I had more wood than we'd need, and as I turned from that glut and took a step toward the house, I felt something gentle–from above the trees that lined the footpath– fall all around me. In the instant, I re-lived the morning, so pregnant with silence, and somehow, by so doing, I half-believed I could move beyond delight or sorrow into stone-quiet, a quiet that might mean consolation.

Sydney Lea

THE KING OF JOKES
for Bruce Richards

At last my soul explodes! "Anywhere! Just so it is out of the world!"
—Charles Baudelaire

Two weeks ago, our four-year-old grandson Mikey sat directly across from me at the Easter dinner table. He picked at the Paschal feast, having predictably defied our caution not to splurge on treats from the annual hunt's artificial eggs: chocolate bunnies, Tootsie Rolls, jelly beans (which he calls *honey beans*), Cheezits, so on.

I can't even glance at that boy, or any of our other seven grandsons and -daughters for that matter, without wanting to give him a prodigious hug.

At his place, Mikey wore a perplexed look. He kept staring into my eyes, muttering "hmmm, hmmm." This briefly disconcerted me, and so did the question he repeated, after two or three minutes: "What *are* you? What *are* you?" Then, all confusion vanished in the instant, he suddenly exclaimed, "I *know*! I *know*! You're the King of Jokes!"

My turn for bemusement. I wasn't in the least put off by the unexpected coronation; I simply didn't know why I deserved it, saturnine as I can too often be. Moreover, although I consider it adequate, maybe more, I don't find my sense of humor superior, say, to my wife's or to his parents', and certainly not to his.

The boy's flamboyant imagination tends toward the surreal. So I was certain, after he scurried away from his chair to play Legos with his older brother, that he was sorting out some wild story to explain my ascent to royalty. Circumstances prevented my hearing that tale at Easter, but it'll come. I know this little fellow.

Another narrative Mikey developed quite a while ago involves the parents he lived with in another world, before being born into this one. He refers to that family's male adult as Uncle Jones.

One of Uncle Jones's primary obligations was to procure game for the household's table, though he'd long since lost a leg in a hunting accident. The man had a curious fashion sense, to call it that: for years, he wore one garment only, an oversized set of boxer underpants, full of holes and covered with polka dots. (I remember thinking, *poor camouflage!*) When, to supplement the family's meager income, he took a part-time job at a restaurant, he chose to wear no clothes at all. Asked if his nakedness perturbed his boss, let alone the customers, Mikey always assures us that "when people eat there, they don't think about anything."

Just after Mikey launched his Uncle Jones saga, my wife asked if there was an Aunt Jones, to which the boy answered, "Yes, Uncle Chris." It seems Uncle Jones's roles were always outdoor ones: fixing the house, butchering hare and deer, building sheds and the like, whereas Uncle Chris tended to indoor pursuits, some practical – cooking, sweeping, making beds– and some more ethereal: painting beautiful pictures (always of ducks), making pottery, writing poems, or simply sitting and thinking. There seem to have been times, too, though not many, when inside and outside activities were switched.

Whether their visit has been short or lengthy, we're always sad to see any of our children and their families leave. On that Easter Sunday, though, as Mikey, his brother, mother, and father departed, for some reason I got lower than ever. I felt neither kingly nor jocular; that was for sure.

It would be easy to ascribe such blues to my advanced age, because in fact I do sometimes lament that I won't have seen as much of these two boys' lives as I have of their older cousins', their parents', uncles' and aunts'. But that's a bald simplism. Watching that car full of loved ones roll down our driveway, I was wistful, yes, but my inward tears betokened fear in addition to sorrow.

Sure enough, next morning the radio would bring news of yet another mass shooting, six dead and eight wounded, some critically. There would follow the usual, contemptible, NRA-sanctioned *thoughts and prayers,* along with the usual shopworn arguments against any sort of firearms control, however vastly our gun-related deaths outnumber those of every other developed nation.

These barbaric shootings, I knew, would continue in the very face of well-established national support for outlawing or at the very least imposing some restrictions on owning military-grade weapons. I shuddered, then cursed to imagine one of our children's children in a spray of bullets from an AK-47 or a Glock. So my soul now contained rage too; it seethed at a level just below the explosive.

My mood led me to the melting of the icecaps, which would go on unabated as aged, white politicians enthusiastically accepted bribes from the fossil fuel complex. Correlatively, more and more lethal plagues and viruses would keep evolving. The fundamental racism of American history and institutions would continue– and its patent existence would be vigorously denied by those most responsible for its perpetuation.

Sydney Lea

The cheerful volubility of the grandchildren and their friends, the frenetic egg hunt, the roast beef supper, and not least the ongoing story of Uncles Jones and Chris– all this had taken my mind off the state of nation and world; but with those loved ones' departure, the horrors to be faced by our grandchildren and their contemporaries besieged me.

So I lay in bed that night, tossed from dread to melancholy to fury, knowing that the idea of any sort of peace amounted to pure delusion, as it always has. Even simple manners would appear quaint in an era to come, when passersby would look back on the inexcusable *Fuck Joe Biden!* signs along some of our neighborhood roads as relatively civil dissent.

In short, every utopian vision we humans have ever mustered would reveal itself, precisely, as a joke. That's the way it's always been, but this time, with the planet in direst peril and its dominant species beset by rage, the punchline would be sublimely terrifying.

There are times, Mikey tells us, when he'd like to go back and live with Uncle Jones. I remind him how I'd miss him. I don't remind him that his otherworldly uncle lost a leg to gunfire, but even if I did, that wouldn't faze him.

Such Dancing as We Can

He's never been shot at. He's never considered the fact that so many innocents like him *have* been fired on and have violently died. Mikey doesn't yet contemplate ruinous weather changes in the making, either, though in time he'll have no choice. Nor does he suspect that his few African American schoolmates and their relatives will suffer disproportionately from the climate crisis, as their parents and ancestors have suffered for centuries from innumerable other calamities, including imperialist wars. The only war the boy cares about for now is the one against evil, waged by Batman, Superman, Spiderman, and the righteous rest whose victory is assured.

What if Mikey *could* imagine the darker issues, as eventually he must? Wouldn't he yearn, as the poet put it, to go anywhere out of the world? Wouldn't the King of Jokes leave his new throne to join him, wherever the boy ended up?

But hell, it was Easter. Our grandson's example of vivid imagination kindled a spark of redemptive dream as I lolled under the bedclothes. As I reach my inconclusive conclusion here, I recall Mikey and that whole gang of ebullient children and I think that miracles– however they strain our pedestrian visions– *can* happen.

Sydney Lea

AMERICAN DREAM
           –for Marjan Strojan

The literary symposium was over for the day. Wanting a bit of time to myself, I went to a pleasant restaurant overlooking Lake Bled, that jewel of Slovenia.

The cuisine was also pleasant, somewhat Latin but something else too, which I can't find language to describe. A stone church guarded a distant bluff and another the water's solitary island, which is in fact the only island in that small, lovely nation. I watched the wooden longboats full of tourists, rowed from abaft by men who leaned and straightened, leaned and straightened. A graceful movement, dance-like.

There on the terrace there was actual dance: a woman singer, one man on Fender bass, another playing some sort of squeezebox, because there always seems to be a squeezebox in this part of the world. I suppose I'd have called their music pleasant too. It found some niche between exuberant techno-pop and the classical stuff derived from folksong, of which the middle-European composers have always been so fond.

There was an old-world melancholy where I sat, for which I appeared, as ever, a sucker. The dancers mostly

Such Dancing as We Can

looked thinner than they would in similar places back home. But then back home there *are* no similar places, really, no dancers who move as these did, with composure and flair at once. It was suddenly easy to dream of bolting my dear country and moving to somewhere like Bled, leaving behind the relative absence of style and civilization, the maddeningly insular frame of mind that doesn't even know there exists somewhere like Bled.

I'd flee all that *stuff*, like those muscle-bound trucks with their oversized U.S. flag decals and their shark-mouth grilles. I'd flee 24-ounce steaks, MAGA, TVs that reach the ceiling at Wal-Mart or Target or Circuit City.

I'd wanted solitude, but instead I felt only lonely.

I had no local language. Yet I did have others. Maybe in time I'd make my way.

All at once, the three musicians played a different music, however awkwardly. The lake downhill remained a gemmy teardrop, and even through the tune I heard the gentle *tong* of the island's bell. The boatmen leaned and rowed as deftly as they did before the mist and the evening settled in. I looked but couldn't see that slip of island.

Sydney Lea

First the band took up "Last Date," all sweet and sour pap– unless like me you remember King Curtis's version on his soprano sax, glissandi flickering, wrenching. That tiny, hole-in-the-wall club. The late great King.

The trio slid unstopping into "Please Release Me." The pretty singer would have killed to be Ray Charles. She failed. Who wouldn't?

I remember thinking how I had those same two bluesy anthems in that same order on my big old pickup's scratchy tape deck forty-odd years before. My love and I, not quite man and wife yet, would creep after dark along the rut-and-gravel roads of our Vermont, notes spilling out the windows. Now I wondered if the thing we call coincidence is real? Be that as it may, I was sick for home, which is what, if you look at its roots, nostalgia means.

My love and I hung on each other close as summer air and sang along with those tunes. Deer peeled off our headlights, thick as mice, and August's moon looked as huge as we could ever dream.

IV. RAGE, IGNORANCE, LOVE

Sydney Lea

IN PRAISE OF IGNORANCE

Having watched a broad-winged hawk coast down from a slab of granite scarp, I chose a certain climb this morning. She or a bird exactly akin returns each spring to nest in our woods, a kind of genius loci; but this was the first I'd seen of her this year.

I can't truly explain why the hawk's descent moved me upward, my pace, of course, slower than once. I recalled more challenging ascents, when at length the forest would turn to scrub, then the ankle-high sprawls of juniper dwindled to nothing. At last even the grasses and mosses disappeared.

But this lower, nearer prominence was also granite-topped, scrimmed only by lichen, whose color, to call it a color, blended all but perfectly with the rock's. I somehow felt a craving for such blankness. That thirst would pass, I knew, but what to make of it now?

Standing on ledge, I inhaled the wind, as if preparing to deliver some oration. I stopped myself, though, conscious that whatever words I used– and I had no idea what they'd be– would be trite at best, and a blasphemy at worst. Whom or what I'd blaspheme also remained obscure, but no one would hear anyhow. Meanwhile, I looked down on a vulture in the valley, mastering air without a flutter, its grace further rebuking my clumsy compulsion to speech.

If what I'd meant to find up there was wisdom, well, maybe I did, though it was of a kind I'd often blundered upon. Why must I learn and re-learn and re-learn the lesson? I mean how little anyone can truly know, and how, having small choice, we should cherish that ignorance. After all, it's what we can be sure we have– or at least it's what I have. Humility demands I acknowledge that truth.

But as it turns out, humble ignorance can comprise both the beautiful and the sublime.

That in itself seemed adequate discovery, or rediscovery. I made my way back down.

Sydney Lea

RAVENS

At dawn, I awakened to ravens, flopping among our window trees like sloppily schooled fish. As they got louder and louder, my annoyance turned to anger.

Geese make a din too when they lift from our pond and head for the river, as they do each morning in the warmer months, almost exactly at 7:00. At least that's a civilized hour, though, and they're out of earshot in a matter of moments. What's more, their flight formation looks military-smart. I know I'm an anthropomorphizing fool, but there was something about the raggedness of the ravens' congregation, both in woods and air, that partly impelled my intemperate scream this morning: *Will you get out of here?* The flock moved perhaps thirty yards north and resumed its chorus.

By now, the morning has mercifully gone cloudy. I can't detect the pine-pollen clouds falling like yellow snow, another thing I'd found to fume at, dust coating our windows and getting into our lungs, so heavy has it been this year.

So it's come down to the birds, who are still at it these hours later, protracting my ugly mood.

Such Dancing as We Can

Suddenly, speaking of birds, the least expected notion touches me like the brush of a wing, though I suppose I'm thinking of less rowdy birds than these. In any case, I abruptly soften. I reason that the higher-pitched and more insistent squalls out there come from this year's young as the mother birds coax them to start life on their own; and I recall what it can be to have shrieking children, how existence can feel downright futile as you seek to guide them in what you consider measured tones– and what somebody else might hear quite otherwise.

I understand that my fury's not with a few irritating scavengers, anyhow, but with the world we creatures share, which teems with horrors, not least the searing complaints of brutalized children. Meek or loud, those innocents' complaints are too often met with abuse, or almost worse, neglect.

And here I've been complaining about some birds' racket and reacting with my own violence, no matter that it's internal.

As if my self-rebuke had charmed them, the ravens, young and grown, wheel off. They scale our ridge, leaving behind them a mild breeze among trees. It rises and ebbs in a rhythm, putting me in mind of peaceful breathing.

Sydney Lea

SHORT TREATISE ON SLOWING DOWN

On the morning of August 20, 2016, I felt a subtle pinch in my upper torso, right side. My wife and I were at our remote cabin in Washington County, Maine, where, among other things, despite my 73 years, I'd been training for a local twelve-mile paddle race. I felt fitter than I had in recent years, when, nonetheless, and despite the fact that the contest was not divided into age classes, I'd consistently finished at or near the head of the flotilla.

The 2016 race, however, was canceled– mercifully, perhaps– for fear of lightning. I felt disappointment, but went about my business. I kept paddling hard, training a young bird dog, chopping wood, and putting things up for the winter in anticipation of our imminent departure for home. I never experienced shortness of breath, no acute pain or crushing sensation, and, but for one very brief and (then) inexplicable moment, no light-headedness. I did feel unusually tired for the ensuing day and a half, and that mosquito-like pinch in my chest persisted.

At length, given that persistence and more importantly my family history –father, grandfather, and great grandfather all dead of coronaries in their fifties– my wife and I decided I should go to the tiny clinic on the New Brunswick border. When, on looking at a blood test, the emergency room doctor informed me I was having a heart attack, I was incredulous. Those were words spoken about other people, not me.

After the three-hour ambulance ride to Bangor and some hours in which the nitroglycerine did not eliminate that little mosquito pinch, I remember being wheeled at what seemed an alarmingly fast clip to some location within the Eastern Maine Medical Center, where a stent would soon be inserted into my 100% occluded right coronary artery.

Sixteen days later, I was in cardio rehab, keeping my heart rate between 125 and 135 for forty minutes at a clip, feeling fitter than before, when I hadn't known a thing was wrong with me. Luckily, damage to the heart did not prove to be radical, and I have felt well ever since. No need for nitro; textbook blood pressure; in short, little to alarm me. Touch wood.

But it's that whirlwind trip to the operating room that I recall most vividly. I can't say I felt terror, because I didn't. It was something else that I can't adequately describe: I can say only that the speed of my world in its spinning unsettled me, to use an imprecise verb. I tried to study things on the corridors' ceilings –a water stain, a light fixture, a sheet rock seam, what have you?– but no sooner did I fix my eye on whatever it was than it vanished.

Sydney Lea

I said while back that I'm one who from his middle years onward has chosen to believe in grace, by which of course I mean unmerited favor. That the opening of the most famous hymn composed by Thomas Dorsey, the father of gospel music, came to mind strikes me in retrospect as oddly unsurprising, though in my all-white, Vermont Congregational church this is not a hymn much heard:

> Precious Lord, take my hand,
> Lead me on, let me stand,
> I am tired, I am weak, I am worn;
> Through the storm, through the night,
> Lead me on to the light...

Yet of course I can't logically account for why "Precious Lord" should have sung itself to me, as it were, in crisis. (If grace were logical, it wouldn't be grace.) Of course, it *is* a famous hymn, and in its rawness and directness, a perfect product of its tragic occasion. Mr. Dorsey, who beforehand had been a fairly prominent purveyor of "devil's music," had confronted the death of his wife Nettie in childbirth, and, within 48 hours, the death of their baby as well. If I too felt tired, weak, and worn, as a blessed husband and father, I literally can't imagine how Georgia Tom, Dorsey's moniker in his bluesman days, must have felt in his far, far more taxing circumstance. He later spoke of how spontaneously the hymn had come to him: he simply started to sing its words.

Somehow, on hearing those very words within my soul (likely in the voice of Mahalia Jackson, who rendered them so movingly at Dr. King's funeral), I did sense that I'd somehow passed through a storm, that light shone ahead. I sensed this chiefly because that full-tilt world had abruptly *slowed down.* Indeed, things now seemed to transpire as if in cinematic slow motion.

This was not, perhaps the greatest instance of grace in my life. That surely occurred when, many years back, I found myself in abiding recovery from alcoholism. I had tried and tried to get away from alcohol and in some measure drugs and never succeeded for any length of time. Then some power greater than my puny little will mercifully intervened.

Those of us who have found sobriety by way of twelve-step programs frequently recite the so-called Serenity Prayer, attributed to Reinhold Niebuhr: *God grant me the serenity to accept the things I cannot change, courage to change the things I can, and wisdom to know the difference.* That this simple and cogent entreaty should have seamlessly introduced itself into the still, small space created by Thomas Dorsey's poignant hymn did not strike me as strange on that gurney ride.

It still doesn't. In many ways, these two prayers— one sung, the other recited— voice the same plea for comfort and resolve. To be sure, as with so many similar moments of clarity, I will forget them for stretches of the time left to me, suppressing that sense of calm and deliberation in favor of whatever idle ends I cling to even in professional retirement. But the contingency of Thomas Dorsey's hymn and Niebuhr's prayer in that hour on that day in that hospital is something that I will always own and can always refer to. I have faith that one or the other or both will be available when I most need them against the helter-skelter of so much human experience.

Such Dancing as We Can

RAGE, IGNORANCE, LOVE
  –in mem. Stephen Arkin (1942-2021)

I. *Rage*

I'd set out on a short hike along a trail our family has trodden clear over decades. I paused for no reason to study an oak– likely not all that young, just slender from having developed, acorn to tree, beneath a canopy of pine. I had unwittingly passed this survivor hundreds of times, no more eye-catching than any random hardwood along that familiar mile, as unremarkable as some stranger's face in a crowd.

But when I looked the little oak over from earth to crown, pondering all that had transpired within its span of life on our land, I swear I foresaw that something inside me would soon be changing. Or did I? I honestly can't say. Memory, even recent, can be a whimsical editor.

In that tree's time, there had been children raised here, grown now, moved on. Not so long before, two had married beside our reed-lined pond, and seven grandchildren, their older siblings' kids, had burst into the world. I have a picture of those youngsters gathered around me, the eyes of each reflecting the candles on my 77th birthday cake.

Sydney Lea

I have raced forward thirty years from my late forties, when we moved cross-river from New Hampshire to this chunk of Vermont. I have moved– no, have hurtled from what I didn't know back then was youth to an age when too many friends are losing hold. My beloved friend Steve, for instance, had been like my own blood from years before my family ever settled here. Now he was fatally ill with duodenal cancer, but the hateful pandemic prevented me from visiting him as his life ebbed.

Suddenly my cell phone rang. A miracle! It works almost nowhere in this rustic region, and if I carry it into the woods at all, it's by mistake. Through her sobs, I caught the voice of my dear friend's daughter. *You have to talk to my dad right now!*

That sentence will live inside me forever.

The disease had drawn its winning card at last. Stunned, I slumped to the ground as he offered his farewell. I envisioned his face as he struggled for words: *This is hard…*

Steve soon stopped for want of breath, and I began a speech I'd been rehearsing for some while– which collapsed, of course, into incoherent blubbering. The call ended when his daughter took the phone again and, choking on her own sorrow, simply breathed, *Good-bye*.

Good-bye indeed– to a man of whom I knew so much: what made him laugh or cry, what music he craved, what food. His every defining physical gesture and turn of phrase were etched into my being. He'd read my poems. I'd read his essays and books, I hope with similar sympathy.

The small oak I'd been contemplating was uninvolved, of course, in Steve's demise, but it would go on living, despite the darkness looming above it, and, enraged by that, I imagined fetching an axe and chopping the damned thing down.

II. *Ignorance*

Next day, despite a mizzling rain, I went in search of that oak, but I carried no axe or saw.

I'd believed the tree would be seared onto my consciousness, but now the puny thing proved difficult to find among so many kindred whips. Something had hidden it from me. Mystified, I tramped back and forth until a sudden wind summoned cracks and groans from the forest. I got a notion. It made no more sense than being enraged by one nondescript tree among thousands. The gale felt like a reprimand for my blaming its disappearance on some invisible agency.

Needless to say too, the idea of some supernal power's rebuking me was absurd. Even if such a fantastical force existed, after all, would it waste time with the meager likes of me or the oakling? And yet, at that very moment, the tree appeared. Was there some magical immanence around me after all?

Who would have thought a tree not much more than head-high could spawn the reactions I had after hearing my treasured friend's waning breaths? Now it had stepped forward again.

What followed was no likelier. Steve and I were college professors for decades, and now my oak unaccountably steered me back fifty years. Racked by nerves, I tried to lead a discussion of Milton's *Paradise Lost*. I telephoned him to report how anxious that teaching assignment had made me. His response was lighthearted: "Can't help you. He's not talking to a Yid like me."

This much later on, I truly absorbed a lesson I'd grasped only by way of intellect in that classroom. During the famous debate in Hell, spirits

> ...fallen from Heaven sat on a Hill retir'd,
> In thoughts more elevate, and reasoned high
> Of Providence, Foreknowledge, Will and Fate,
> Fixt Fate, free will, foreknowledge absolute,
> And found no end, in wand'ring mazes lost.

Such Dancing as We Can

I'd be in for hellish confusion myself should I start, like those idiot devils, to ponder ultimate things. And it had been madness, particularly, to resent a mere tree.

III. *Love*

I sat on the stump of a yellow birch that I had in fact cut down for firewood a decade before, and I watched my oak completely shed the guilt I'd preposterously assigned to it. The stiff breeze purged the mist, and the trunk's surface, bathed now in sun, burst into every hue of the spectrum, from red at the base to violet at the crown. I didn't imagine such transformation. I beheld it.

A cluster of mushrooms gathered around the trunk was also swathed in brilliance, and another memory supervened. At a certain New Haven diner in our first graduate school days, we ordered mushroom omelets one Sunday morning. The waitress, perhaps as old as I am now, asked, *caps or stems?* We sensed a wryness: eyebrows lifted, she was poking subtle fun at the eatery's affectation in offering such a choice. Every time Steve and I returned to that place, we'd wait for however long it took for one of her tables to be free. And we never varied our orders– caps, of course– just as she, clearly amused, never altered the rite.

Or rather she did– just once. After a summer's absence from town, we sat at our usual spot. Then we waited for what seemed a full minute. The woman mutely stood there, thin as a blade, pad and pencil quivering in her hand. Her eyes held not a smile but bone-weariness and pain.

At uncomfortable length, in chorus, we said *caps*.

That was the last time we saw her. We'd later learn of her own cancer.

And next I recalled another 1960s moment, the two of us high on home-grown weed. Just before we headed off to some much-lauded visiting scholar's lecture, we'd been listening to Muddy Waters's "Long Distance Call." The visitor was gushingly introduced, but before he could begin his talk, Steve stood and shouted the song's raunchy double-entendre: *Another mule is kickin' in your stall!*

The outburst was so utterly out of context in that highbrow hall that no one knew how to respond, and no one did. After a long pause, the lecture simply began, but by then Steve and I were laughing our way out the door. We called each other Muddy ever after.

These random memories had no special value– except that they did and do. Like all the others.

Once again, I invoked Milton's ruined devils. How could I possibly have foretold that their fervent philosophical blather would constitute an anti-ideal for me as Stephen Arkin lay dying in California?

Such Dancing as We Can

I'd waste no strength on conjecture. I'd discover no justification for so shattering a loss. Instead, my thoughts moved from Milton's fallen angels to his human beings—likewise fallen, just as Steve was, I am, everyone of us is.

> The World was all before them, where to choose
>
> Thir place of rest, and Providence thir guide:
> They hand in hand with wandring steps and slow,
> Through Eden took thir solitarie way.

The oak still clung to its polychromatic glow.

Sydney Lea

Sunday Noons

Having bought a Sunday paper, I stood sipping coffee in our village store, absently staring through the plate glass window onto the street. I was conscious of my neighbors' affable palaver all around me. I couldn't catch specifics of any conversation but I didn't really try.

I crave such brief and peaceful moments these days, when somehow little seems of great importance. I savor the flow of the ordinary. That day I even felt content with the weather, which was scarcely the stuff of postcards or calendars: late winter's gray, the mud-soiled dregs of old snow melting along the ditches into paltry runoff.

I wouldn't have guessed it, but our little byway had kept a very few widespread patches of ice. Fate intruded, if that's what you'd call it, and a stranger decided to touch her brakes precisely on one of those slicks and slued into the one tree anywhere nearby. A yard farther on and she'd have been safe.

You know how it is after shock. You can't quite size things up right away. It's like touching a strand of fence-wire that you hadn't known was electrified. I stood unmoving a long, long time before going out to my truck and heading home the long way. From my house a mile uphill, I heard shrieks from ambulance and cruiser sirens.

Such Dancing as We Can

Later, we'd learn the driver had died before reaching the clinic. I'd seen just her head as she lay against her window, almost as if she were napping. Or rather I glimpsed it before I looked away. A bird's-foot bloodstain on her scalp would lodge itself in my brain, but not the driver's features, so briefly had I looked on. I picture the ditchwater more clearly, dark as bock beer. What an odd image to retain.

To be sure, I felt sick, and felt my damnable helplessness, but although that crash happened years ago, I also recall a strange nostalgia as I drove away, an unaccountable memory completely unrelated to the horror I'd witnessed. What prompted it? I have no idea.

What could it mean that the memory arrived immediately after they hauled the victim off? I'll never know. With each passing year, I'm further resigned to what an ocean of things I'll never know. In the times I fetched back, bloodshed at worst meant knees scraped raw if we fell off our bikes. No one we cared about had died yet.

And we knew some wonders: our dad had restored a Model T Ford, which he shifted with pedals. All of us children would clamor for drives as soon as the weather turned mild. For whatever reason, I found myself in that Ford again, along with my brothers and sisters and my father, still so gentle, so young, so *alive*.

Sydney Lea

Undying, they seemed, those springtime Sundays, June's pastorale unscrolling itself, each tree we passed spring-laden with leaves, a few lush clouds above, a flock of crows flapping lazily by, hay still standing in emerald fields, white clusters of clover on either side of the road.

Such Dancing as We Can

WHAT TIME WAS IT?

That long-legged woman was not you, though she was almost as striking, almost as tall. We stood together for mere moments on the sidewalk, having come out of a Rothko exhibit. The paintings were hung on one floor only. How had I missed her indoors?

She seemed rushed. I saw her hail a taxi and flee, as I inanely put it to myself. In that mere instant, I noticed her beauty, but although they never met mine, it was more specifically her eyes that intrigued me. Unlike yours, they seemed full of sadness.

She shook out her hair just before getting into the cab. The gesture was brisk, but it made me sigh, because it too revealed certain fascinating, if indefinable traits, ones I now know were of my own invention.

Tell me my sorrow at her disappearance was plain silly, and I can't argue, yet to a desperately romantic and lonesome young man it felt profound.

Music, cuisine, dance styles, fashions and a million further things have changed since she escaped, as I absurdly put it that May afternoon. But just after she rode off, I turned– and there you were. Of course, you weren't, not for years, but my interior time is forevermore elastic.

Sydney Lea

You were there, and, incredibly, still are. Thank God the other woman got free so quickly, I say to myself, no matter nothing indicated she gave me a passing thought as someone to be dodged– or even noticed.

If there's a god, then he or she or it uses coincidence to get things accomplished while remaining incognito. That putative deity forced my paragon's rapid retreat, and prompted a number of other things. Otherwise, you and I would never have met.

I'd been offered that job in the northwest, had even been sent the airplane ticket to come look around the college campus. A day before going, though, I got an offer in upper New England and accepted it. What might life down in New York be like for you? Or Charleston? Or San Francisco? That's the sort of thought you may have been entertaining in those days. You had so many capacities, as you'd go on to prove, and I'm sure the opportunities would have been legion.

We two are together, four decades later. How right in hindsight, that taxi cab's speeding away.

At one point, I saw the young woman examine her wrist, which was naked. How right in hindsight, her not asking me, say, what time it was.

Such Dancing as We Can

SUPERNAL

 –*supernal–* adjective mainly literary relating to the sky or the heavens; celestial. • of exceptional quality or extent: *he is the supernal poet of our age | supernal erudition.*
–New Oxford American Dictionary

The sky showed leaden with the prospect of rain. I'd been at it long enough that I'd called myself poet for some time without the embarrassment and self-doubt that once made me cringe. But Lord knows I have never imagined myself supernal, nor construed the poetic life as coterminous with wisdom.

I was just a man running errands.

 As I drove, I'd been reminiscing again on our family's move from a hamlet whose every dirt and paved byway I could drive without thought to one in which I was obliged to start all over. That was a shockingly long time back.

Now I followed a narrow lane in this other quarter. Sudden sunlight burst through and struck the dingy plow-drifts of March. I watched three robins fossick in gravel. A scent of wet earth came in through my slightly cracked window.

Sydney Lea

These oddments reminded me of when I first figured out this shortcut from a nearby town's gas station to its grocery store, a route well known to anyone who's lived mere months here but of course brand new to me then. I recalled how such small discovery felt revelatory.

By now I've driven the cut-off for decades, but it broke on me like that very sun: *I'm here!*

Well, of course, I thought with a smile, unseen by anyone else, we all have to be somewhere.

Many, I knew, rejoice in their own good luck– maybe not at unpredicted luster on remnant Vermont snow or a few unexceptional birds or a whiff of dirt, but at the morning glow on a church's stone in Québec, say, or clouds that swarm above the Serengeti, a green sky in the Solomons… I stopped myself from going on.

But *supernal:* yes, it seemed wondrous, even uncanny, that just then, of all earth's numberless places, the one where I happened to live should belong to *me* as my years ran down.

But so it did– and so much of it still new.

Such Dancing as We Can

MORE THAN FACT

I've kicked all the way through this unkempt yard to find the stone for my uncle's housemaid, hidden by tall grass and weeds. At last I've found it.

I can't, though, find a counterpart to that touchy uncle's *bachelor* for Mary Griffin. *Spinster?* I'd choke on that one, though she surely knew worse injustice in Belfast, Catholic girl in her mostly mad-Prod nation.

I hadn't planned to start these reflections by censuring the inequities that left her harassed, unpraised, and in the end forgotten. I only meant to discover this modest marker. After all, the abuse she encountered, followed by virtual disappearance, is all too sadly common. As Shelly has famously reminded us in "Ozymandias," even memories and relics of the great and empowered crumble with astonishing speed.

I've never come to this cemetery before, I'm ashamed to say. I've been that ungrateful. And, truth be told, I visit now as much to fetch back scenes that comforted me as I do to pay homage. I'm a relatively unscathed man by almost anyone else's standards, but, over the sixty and some years that Mary's been gone, like all of us I've seen my share of death and grief. So it still soothes me that I can picture her, say, as she rocks in a chair, having tended to her volatile boss's end-of-day demands. And to mine.

I catch the faintest hum as she embroiders things she'll send to relatives in Ireland, children she's never seen and won't. I'm astonished to recall how such gentle magnanimity could actually make me jealous. It was only that, come the weekend, I didn't want to share any part of her sustaining warmth, which was sometimes lacking at home. That's a fact, though I'm well past blaming anyone, including myself, for those circumstances.

I'd later also understand Mary's goodness in keeping me ignorant of how those rabid neighbors bullied her childhood. At least they did so by my best guess. I have no other recourse than assumption: she never allowed herself to reminisce out loud about any personal trials, and when I complained about what I construed as my own, she indulged me, consoled me.

I hope that a boy's callow self-pity was less than sinful.

Another instance: I can all but hear the machine that separated the cow herd's milk from the sweet cream I'll sample after its rattling quits and after I've finished the supper she'll make for us two.

Such Dancing as We Can

Then off to sleep. As darkness nears, I summon the bedtime songs she sang to me in Gaelic, whose meanings were obscure, or so I thought– like the bits of prayer and chant that steal from the church over there, where she knelt at five each morning while I lay snug beneath my eiderdown.

Like the more important meanings of those old songs, I choose to believe that those muffled sounds I hear as I pause in the graveyard offer a greater truth for being hazy, for containing more than fact.

I want to believe they imply a notion, imprecise but vivid, that I still cling to, however naïvely: that beside the world of grief and bigotry that's so overwhelmingly familiar, there may be another where selfless love can thrive.

Sydney Lea

HAZE

During the corona crisis I indulged myself in various ways. No matter I'd trod the planet for a long time and half a decade past had logged that one coronary event in one hospital's records, say, I cooked up bacon and eggs each Sunday morning.

On one of those Sundays, I looked up from the skillet and out onto the yard, where I found a purple finch, a clot of wild iris, a hop hornbeam still in rare bloom, a boulder striated with red quartz, and a rock maple whose leaves seemed exorbitantly large, given the youth of the tree.

I recognized– it's the sort of revelation I'm frequently offered and as frequently forget– that I'd too often taken such splendors for granted. Feeling somewhat ashamed, then, I summoned the same old goad: *You have one life to live.*

Breakfast could wait. I killed the heat. My wife had left bed well before me, eaten, and gone out hiking. I decided to take my own hike, but only around the house. I meant to proceed deliberately.

A living room window looks downhill onto the patch of playground we fashioned when our kids were a lot

Such Dancing as We Can

younger. As I gazed through the glass, a puff of breeze bent the weeds at the playground's verges and set a swing in ghostly motion.

Next, I opened the door to the front porch and gazed through screens, which blurred our pond and the beach that we also made back then, overtaken since by blackberry cane and bindweed.

I watched a snapping turtle slog onto what remained of the beach's sand to drop and bury her eggs, despite the fact that the day was raw, as many had been that June, a local phenomenon that, like all their kind elsewhere, the area's science deniers will cite when they scoff at what is lazily called global warming. Of course, we'd also seen temperatures in the mid-90s, and, though I am scarcely a scientist myself, nowadays I suspect that anything historically unusual is likely a portent of crisis.

I remembered when cedar waxwings clouded that same pond at certain easily predicted intervals during this month, various ephemerids hatching from it as if on cue. No birds or bugs that morning.

The night before, my wife and I had lit the woodstove. Now I watched her graceful, tall shape emerge from the woods.

Sydney Lea

A haze of smoke, rather than rising as it should have in
such a chill, sheathed the lawn like gossamer.

Such Dancing as We Can

AFTER THE HEAT WAVE
 —for Tony Whedon

I study the light of late afternoon on the ridge. My wife and I can observe it from our porch, to which we would migrate like palmers last week, after the heat of the day had grudgingly loosened its grip. What then resembled the hue of an infertile yolk now earns the acclamatory cliché: golden.

It's late August, the dark arriving earlier by the day. But what's time? We have old people's leisure. During that awful hot spell, now happily past, we could soak in the pond downhill until we were cool.

Now a small bunch of starlings crosses the waning sun– like sprinkled pepper, I think, revealing my cureless affection for trope, for which I mildly upbraid myself. After that sapping siege, this restorative scene is sufficient in its own right. It scarcely needs my adornment. And yet I can't really make myself repent. A person of my age is all done with becoming; and would I change what at last I turned into anyhow? Maybe not.

On this fine Saturday, each feature of our little domain– that gilding light, the barely detectable hint of lilac on the breasts of two doves pecking driveway gravel, the way even the field's nuisance burdocks seem comely as a breeze troubles their leaf-heavy stalks— calls for celebration.

How I luxuriated last night in pulling up quilts. As the temperature floats around 60 degrees. I scarcely recall my clothes hanging dank, the Saharan feel of dust on the lane from house to town road. And today I hiked through the woods at a pace that vaguely resembled brisk. The cooler weather elevated my mood, just as the infernal had invited searing reflections. One of my oldest and most cherished friends was no longer in this world. It seemed astonishing! Another friend, reliant on doctors, or by now on God, clove to thin hope that something miraculous could be done for him. *If I'm dying,* he wrote in late winter, *I won't tell another soul.* His gallows humor seemed only tragic during the heat wave.

He got well. Then his wife died.

Now the two doves fly off together. Despite the breeze and my poor hearing, I detect the faint whistle of their wings. Shadows stretch across the field, whose green yields first to bronze, then suspends itself on the cusp of black. Night-birds tune their throats and tiny frogs prepare their tireless songs.

I conjure what I couldn't feel in our recent inferno, namely gratitude for the love of place, and even more, as

Such Dancing as We Can

so very often, for the love of a three-generation family and of steadfast friends, quick and dead, who have salved my despair, as entirely unearned as the fondness they've lent me, and who have shared in my delights as well.

This cool will deepen, will guide me into the night.

Sydney Lea

THE WATER LOT

We'll never see the likes of our neighbor Tink again: men from this part of the world who went to work full-time in the woods or on the farm just out of eighth grade, laboring by muscle power alone, and who kept their families and hired help and chickens all fed, the houses warm, clothes made and repaired.

We lost Tink four winters ago. He was 97.

Stories were the common currency in lumber camp, kitchen, and barn. Tink, who began logging at 13 years old and weighing 108 pounds, shared a lot of those tales with our family.

I'm thinking today of a place he called the Water Lot, where early citizens sought a way to supply the village. The lot lies at the base of a very sheer incline, and the descent and ascent make for the most strenuous nearby hike I know. Depressions still show down there in the bowl, chopped with mattocks and wedges from the limestone cap in the late nineteenth century, even before our old neighbor's time.

Along with a few lengths of lead pipe, the holes are all that's left. The effort was abandoned, according to what Tink learned as a boy, after very little water was

Such Dancing as We Can

discovered, and such as there was no good, reeking of iron and sulfur. *Same way Hell smells, pretty likely,* Tink said with his trademark rogue's half-smile.

It's worth a detour to note that the water source they did eventually find lies high on a hill five miles from town, and that local men got together to dig six foot trenches from there to the village and to each of its houses, *all in the summer and early autumn of 1915.*

Sometimes it's emphatically clear to me that I've never worked hard, even when I've had what I thought were bone-wearying jobs.

What is gone, like our ancient neighbor's archaic diction, like those meager excavations— whatever's faded, failed, or derelict— may turn picturesque with age. Consider, say, Roman or Mayan ruins, the Temples of Angkor Wat.

No one, of course, will arrange travel excursions to the Water Lot. It's not on so grand a level, except to the tiny number, maybe me alone, who love it precisely for being so remote and hidden.

Few ever stoop to inspect those muddy holes in our time, apart from some hunter or animal, perhaps a moose in spring who sniffs at some paltry puddle, then ambles on to the freshet on the sidehill. However ungainly the beast is, it has some elegance there.

Of course, *there* is my own construction, as is the moose.

Even into my early sixties, I'd scamper down to the lot and hike up again at a pace that stuns me in retrospect. Now I pause for caution at every outcrop going down, and the same for respite coming back. There's some advantage to this pace in that I sometimes notice things more thoroughly, or I hope so.

But just now I'm recalling something inexplicable. Not long ago, headed downward, I was sure I heard a cry in the hollow, a seemingly human one. A surge hot as solder shot through my soul. Near-perfect silence followed, hardly interrupted by whispers of breeze in the understory. That quiet unnerved me above all– can I put this adequately?– because it distilled the prior sound. No, I can't find words to explain myself.

I continued even more warily for a while but in due course I puttered around the Water Lot for half an hour, always with that eerie feeling that someone might be watching. From one edge to the other, however, I found no human track, no evidence of struggle or blood or presence of any kind.

Such Dancing as We Can

I sat on a windfall spruce, trying to make my mind as empty as one of those forsaken pits. Yet I had no defense against the notion that the awful sound had come from somewhere deep within *me,* perhaps in protest of a pain whose meaning gets clearer every year.

I come to the Water Lot to bring back Tink and a few others like him. But even if unawares, surely I'm also searching– as futilely as the old timers did for water here– of a younger self. Maybe he'd put up a more vigorous fight against becoming a ruin himself, a scattering of relics that unknown successors might find.

Suppose they did, though. They'd fetch back nothing sublime.

Sydney Lea

Oko

 I smacked my foot against a table leg this morning and scolded myself: *Watch where you're going!* A blood-bead stood below the nail, whose jaundiced color puzzled our grandson, here for the weekend. He asked, "Grandpa, how come you're gold?"

But he quickly turned his attention to that little globe of blood. Our interest in pain, or so it seems to me, develops early. We may take whatever measures we can to avoid it and yet it intrigues.

I recall, for instance, a hornet's stinging that child's older brother a summer ago. The two still speak of the incident now and then. The pains, or rather for the most part griefs, that hold my own attention now tend to be psychological rather than bodily, however hard they often are to identify exactly.

This grandson of ours owns a little plush dog named Oko for whatever reason, and the child loves to say he's been stolen by what he calls *billains*. Or sometimes the dog's simply lost. I know it's feigned, yet I still wince at his look, precisely, of pain.

Oko's never gone for long, however, and I rejoice with the boy when he's found.

Such Dancing as We Can

Speaking of loss, at my age I'm losing friends, some to the Reaper, some to scrambled brains. I wish I could find *them* again, celebrate their return. One of the brightest men I've known, for instance, an estimable poet and critic, is now so overwhelmed by multiple sclerosis that he can barely talk, let alone move; another longtime friend, this one Irish, a man with whom I've shared woe, delight, and absurdist humor for decades, is in a seaside institution, and doesn't even know my name; two springs ago, dear Steve, marathon runner, non-smoker and -drinker, my boon companion for well over half my life– himself contracted irremediable cancer of the duodenum and was gone in less than twelve months. The list seems all but infinitely extensible.

As for me, at last I've become my family's oldest member, apart from two of my own first cousins I haven't seen in decades. Both my grandparents and parents, one brother, all my aunts and uncles are long since gone. So when Oko disappears and our grandson expects me to make a sorrowful face, I do have resources.

I struggle against dwelling on my own mortality. I don't always prevail, but when I do arrive at a saner frame of mind, I conclude that so long as I'm not dead, I'm alive. Instead of trying to reckon how long I'll keep them, I concentrate on my capacious good fortune.

Of course, a fact I hope I haven't overly harped on, I'm experiencing natural physical decline, but I can still hike, row my shell, paddle canoe and kayak, and in fact do pretty much what I've always done, at whatever rate. My short-term memory is not what it was, but I can still write and think pretty clearly (at least I *think* I can). A subtle bittersweetness has taken up permanent residence in my soul, but far better that than dejection

Before we carry him up to bed, our grandson, plush dog in hand, dictates words to us for a postcard we'll send to his mother and father and that hornet-stung brother.

Grandpa's toes are gold. Today he bleeded. I lost Oko but Grandpa found him. He's happy.

Such Dancing as We Can

ON WEEPING

On a November day just after Thanksgiving, a year before a virus arrived to change the world, I remember noticing a grandson's boot in a dark corner of our dining room, where he must have kicked it off. Somehow his parents had left it behind when they went home.

How *little* it was! And how little I could find to complain about, old man who's seen less tragedy and ill fortune than most. But I instantly recalled a morning many, many years before, when my lifelong friend Don dropped by. Following their divorce, his ex-wife had moved with their children to another state. After they'd gone, he told me how he cried on finding his son's small toothbrush in his medicine cabinet.

I thought I understood back then. I'm married for good, please God, and for me this is scarcely a time of hardship. Still, I understand those feelings of Don's a lot better now. That tiny boot made me weep.

Tears come more freely as my years accumulate and dwindle. For whatever reason, I keep referring to Fats Domino. When Fats died a few Octobers back, for instance, I spoke on the phone with that friend of decades who died himself two springs ago. Like me, he still delighted in a certain kind of music we craved in

Fats's time. We sniffled over his passing and reminisced, and thanked our stars that the man and some others had delivered us from Ricky Nelson, Georgia Gibbs, Pat Boone, Teresa Brewer, and the like.

I now and then find myself singing in poor imitation: *We happy in my blue heav-awn.* Fats's rendition was the first rock 'n' roll .45 I ever bought. On hearing it one morning, my poor hung-over mother blurted, "What in the world is *that?*" Well, what it was not, to her clear disgust, was the Tin Pan Alley version she knew, all strings and lilies and light.

Just now I drink up the sun through our kitchen window. On such bright days, northern New England's November can be exquisite, the naked land like a woodcut, its mountains' contours chiseled. But let even one cloud come to block that light and my tears stand by– which I guess isn't hard to explain. On the other hand, come to think, sunshine can bring them on too.

Our nest is empty. How we loved the five children and, needless to say, still do. But the girls are women, and our boys have long since grown their beards more quickly than I can now. I am far beyond mere happiness that they have their own children, all living quite near. They're often at our house, in fact, though the COVID pandemic imposed unwelcome limits on that sort of thing. We missed half of the youngest one's then two years of life in that epoch of quarantine.

I remembered sitting amidst all those children and grandchildren on that last family Thanksgiving, here at the table where I've chosen to write this. I look over, and it's as though that small boot still stares at me from its nook.

With the qualified defeat of the plague, or what we're cautiously led to believe is a defeat, I pray the assemblies of our sprawling clan will proliferate once again. With every get-together, this place will be a mess. I feel only joy to imagine havoc again, litter of toys and games, furniture bullied askew, small footwear kicked off in haste. I look forward to young parents dancing with their sons and daughters to music whose pleasures I'm too old to fathom. But I too will do as much of such dancing as I can.

I'll see all this, no doubt, with blurred vision.

Sydney Lea

ABIDING BEAUTY

When we were boys, we called it The Cabin, though by then it had things that on buying the place our grandfather had lacked: light, heat, plumbing, telephone– all the modern rest.

Its little lake was full of sunfish. They were easily fooled, though when we three brothers caught them, they looked too bright to kill. As kids, we didn't use terms like *loveliness* but we grasped the idea of it and threw our catch back more often than not.

Years later, I, the eldest, sit in the parking lot of a huge box store; I'm waiting for my wife to emerge with supplies for our own cabin, more than five hundred miles north of Grandpa's, a place as close as I'll ever come to that childhood one, with its carefree summers, its lake and ridge, all of which I still invoke as paradigms of worldly welcome.

I have stayed in the car to keep an eye on our three dogs, who crowd the backseat. They are as eager as I am to be somewhere else but they'll stay patient– unlike the woman whose words I just heard through my half-open rear window. She barked at her husband, *You don't call me beautiful no more!* Then, swinging her tote bag almost like a weapon, she scurried away from him. Because he had a severe limp, the poor man couldn't catch up. As she fled, he called to her *I do! I do!* like a wheezed reiteration of an old wedding vow.

Where and how do they live, those two, I wonder? That man's about my age, so I feel both curiosity and an instinctive sympathy, though I know I can have no insight into their relationship.

When we three boys sat on the dam at The Cabin, those fish nipped our toes. I have motives

to think of such precious moments as heat shimmers over this asphalt expanse. The dogs keep panting, but not from that heat alone.

It strikes me, as it has so often, how little a person can see of the future: one of us brothers dying in his thirties or two sisters' coming after the boyhood I'm reminiscing about. Nor would I have dreamed up a sprawling, crowded place like this. There was no way for a young boy– or anyone, really– to predict that one day I'd perform these mental leaps from cabin to cabin. It would have been impossible to conceive of marriage, and especially to imagine a wife to whom I'd be so devoted, or any wife at all.

Sydney Lea

But I see mine coming out of that mammoth store. Her shopping bag is full and heavy, and I leap out to take it from her. As I approach, she smiles, this four-decade love of my life, willowy, tall, and as winsome as ever.

I tell her out loud: *You're beautiful.*

Such Dancing as We Can

After First Snow

> *Even for the least division of an hour*
> *Have I been so beguiled as to be blind.*
> 　　–William Wordsworth, "Surprised by Joy"

I remember the day very well, one of those I periodically experience in which I wonder what my life has ever been about. No real reason for it: I just felt a discomfiting lack of purpose. That's an abiding condition for some retirees, and I'm lucky that I experience it so rarely.

That day, I was on an errand to the market one town south. A couple dear to us needed some groceries, both of them down with the flu. I intended my puny service to be a way out of my self-preoccupation.

It was a Friday afternoon, and shoppers crowded the supermarket, readying for the weekend. It demoralized me to see people doing their dull, fruitless chores, the same ones I'd been doing all these years.

The car radio had testified to the sick state of the world. This was over a year back, and no matter the president, a patent crook, and his whole vile crew of lying toadies denied it, our one and only earth was catching fire. Ensuing news reports were almost as dismaying.

Sydney Lea

Under my breath, I hissed, *It's one big shit-show if you ask me.* Of course no one had, but that scarcely slowed me down. In my late-autumn ennui I invoked Ecclesiastes, itself not a terribly original gesture. *The thing that hath been, it is that which shall be; and that which is done is that which shall be done; and there is no new thing under the sun.*

Amen, thought I.

Inside the store, I caught myself passing judgment on everything from clothes to speech to conduct. I knew I should censure myself for such arrogance, and yet nothing seemed innocent enough that, blinded by my fetid *Weltschmerz*, I'd spare it my cynical assessment.

As I made my way toward home, my gloom felt almost delectable. Halfway, I looked out onto our postcard-gorgeous river valley, concluding that it was far too late for astonishment. Mount Moosilauke thrust itself up in the distance, its granite contours carved sharp by boreal air and white with the prior night's snowfall, first of the year. In my mood, everything in that panorama, even that magisterial mountain, had become unexceptional.

Or almost everything. A shaft of sun broke through the overcast, such that a wide and lustrous swath of orange flamed in the foreground.

Such Dancing as We Can

It was made of small pumpkins left for seed in a riverside field– whose color now seemed to imbue the world with a refreshing glow, one never before been seen on earth, by me or anyone else.

Sydney Lea

REST AND BEAUTY

She's gone now, and well spared, but I'm still sad to recall our last moments together.

Her wits all blighted, she didn't recognize me, although she'd been my friend for more than sixty years. Our birth dates are mere days apart.

With so little to offer, I dreaded those occasional visits. Conscience and habit were what brought me there to hear her disorderly, ceaseless monologue, that final time a mishmash of prayers. It was tempting simply to ignore the chatter, but I waited, vainly longing for some small burst of coherence.

Meanwhile, having casually examined a skein of family snapshots on her nightstand, my eyes stopped at a plate hung on one of the walls. It bore the crude likeness of a loon, a few dots of white here and there on a blue background suggesting star-dappled water. Where is it now, I wonder? Likely cleared away with the rest of what her children doubtless regarded as bric-a-brac.

The moon on the plate was imperfectly round. Its hue and shape roughly matched a smooth pebble that sat, unaccountably, amid the photographs, which may well be

Such Dancing as We Can

gone now too. She'd probably plucked the stone from her hometown's spectacular lakeshore in happier times.

Like the kitchen and the common room, even in later fall her room felt humid; but that dankness in fact had prevailed throughout the seasons.

Prompted by a whiff of urine, I recalled a wretched boyhood moment. My mother chaired the House of Rest, a church-sponsored old ladies' home, or, in the decorous patois we've developed since, an assisted-living community. Despite my vehement objection, she ordered me to play my harmonica for the residents on Christmas Eve.

I blundered through Stephen Foster's "Old Folks at Home," entirely unaware, mere child that I was, of the tune's racist implications. My mother likely didn't think about such a matter, so familiar was the song in those days; but shouldn't she at least have recognized that its very title might be ill suited to a place like that? If I'd been able to think such things through myself, I'd have had even greater motive to escape from the piss and blather; from liverish, juddering hands that chucked my chin; from simple chagrin at my painfully inept performance.

Toward the end of our final visit, though she made no more sense than before, my old friend suddenly turned chirpy, as if she were gossiping again with other young mothers on brief leave from their domestic concerns. On Saturdays long before, they used to assemble for lessons from an impoverished ceramicist, known chiefly for his heavy drinking. My friend often told me how melodramatically teary the poor fool could become even as he was supposed to be offering instruction, though she spoke of his failings with her typical charity. It was in one of those Saturday sessions, I suppose, that she made the plate with its loon, its stars, its glittering water, its distorted moon.

I fended off my own tears, which weren't melodramatic. At least I hope not. They came on as I considered every human's pitiable efforts, great and small, bumbling and often exhausting, to conjure beauty– and to feel at rest.

Such Dancing as We Can

WHAT THE SMART PEOPLE THINK
–for Dr. John Wylie

Let me start by quoting a song written for George Jones in the 1990s by Nashville veterans Randy Boudreaux, Sam Hogin, and Kim Williams:

> I started drinking and actin' crazy
> Way back in '65
> Mama would pray and say, he's my baby
> Lord, please keep him alive
>
> Sister came home with two little children
> Her man had left her alone
> Mama knew too well the hurt she was feelin'
> Cause daddy had been gone so long
>
> We all did our part to add to her pain
> We all broke her heart but she never complained
>
> She loved a lot in her time
> She watched love grow and die on the vine
>
> She stood in the shadows
> So others could shine
> She loved a lot in her time

In due course, the song reports that Mama's prayers are answered: George has sobered up, his sister has remarried to "a good ol' boy– they don't live far from here," and Mama herself has "gone on home." So the tale concludes:

> The words in our hearts
> Are engraved on her stone:
> *She loved a lot in her time.*

What I have to say here– not so oddly at all, as I hope to show– has been spurred by this song, which, the last few mornings, I've found myself singing when I wake up, trying and of course failing to catch the late country star's inimitable "high lonesome" intonations.

I'll get back to such a matter, but I need to provide some back-story, which may at first seem unconnected.

For one who spent all his professional life in rather tony English departments, I'm a person whose literary education has been pretty spotty. Whatever my secondary school's virtues, by and large they did not include its English teachers. These men were not "literary" in any way I would later be expected, and would pretend, to be.

One of those teachers was an affable but extremely lazy southern gentleman who assigned a lot of papers but read them with little care if he read them at all. Indeed, my clique of friends often inserted wise-guy asides into our texts to prove his lack of rigor. I recall one of my own: *If you get this far, Mr. M, I'll buy you a steak sandwich.* None of us was ever found out.

I pulled my most outrageous prank in a sophomore term paper, whose subject was a much under-noticed 19th-century author named Erwin Fiske. I quoted at length from his voluminous and once-popular work, and I ended with the ardent hope that his consignment to literary oblivion might be remedied.

This proved, alas, a vain hope, but only because Mr. Fiske's disappearance into pure obscurity came of his nonexistence. The author, along with all the works I cited, was a product of my own subversive device.

M nonetheless rewarded me with an A and, in his final remarks, commended me for my hopes for Fiske's resurrection, which he claimed to share. I'm sure he simply skipped from page one of my screed to the final page, got the gist, and slapped on the metaphoric gold star.

The best of my English teachers, Mr. A, to whom I do owe a considerable debt, made no real pretense of being a belletristic type. He'd been a journalist for years, and thus owned a keen eye for the sort of filler and froth with which I liked to lace my prose (as in unguarded moments I fear I still can).

One valuable thing Mr. A did was to invite various members of the community into the classroom so that we students could interview them. Wisely, the teacher did not limit these guests to the allegedly distinguished in the neighborhood: we were as apt to query the janitor as the bank president. We not only had to prepare our questions but also to write up articles on these sessions by the very next class meeting.

The true virtue of studying with Mr. A, then, was that he had us write and write– and write some more; but he was also scrupulous and deft in his critiques. Gilded b.s. was the flavor of the day when we wrote for Mr. M, but Mr. A wanted lucidity and concision. He once told me he saw nothing wrong with the theme I'd given him that couldn't be rectified by a simple procedure. "Find a stiff scrub brush," he counseled, "use it, and let me see the results tomorrow."

Practice made perfect. Or no, not perfect, but, thanks to A, practice gave me sufficient mastery of exposition that I placed into an advanced English course when I entered college. It was an excellent survey, taught by a professor named James Boulger, who for whatever reason did not make the tenure cut at Yale in subsequent years.

Such Dancing as We Can

Together, we considered Chaucer, Spenser, Milton, Pope, Wordsworth and Eliot in that order.

I labored for a spell to find the sophisticated critical manner (in most cases, more stylistic than substantial) of my prep school-trained peers, but I did very well with that curriculum, and to this day, I feel I know these six poets as well as I do most writers in the anglophone canon.

I continued to take English courses and to do honors and high honors work in them, but I had no grand design, no strategic path toward command of literary history, themes or techniques. I assumed that such a path would be laid out for me once –at the end of sophomore year– I declared as an English major.

Which, as it turns out, I did not. At the last minute, under the influence of a charismatic senior I admired, I elected a special divisional honors program. It was, essentially, an intellectual history sequence, arranged by units: I remember a fascinating one called "Vienna, 1900," for example, in which we considered the paintings of Klimt and Schiele, the music of Mahler, the pioneering texts of Freud, the appalling *Mein Kampf,* and so on. We sought – rather presumptuously, in retrospect– to arrive at synthetic views of crucial moments in the evolution of culture. (We were not advised, as we would rightly have

262

been some decades later, to remember that it was *western* culture we examined.)

Come senior year, each of us chose an honors thesis topic. I wrote a rambling paper on the gifted, fascistical French novelist Louis-Ferdinand Céline. This was an intriguing but perhaps eccentric choice, as I see it now.

After graduation, and a one-year stint of teaching English and French in a private school, a job that felt far too taxing to pursue for a day longer than that, and, frankly, by way of ducking the new war in Viet Nam that had already killed one of my college roommates, I decided to go to graduate school.

Virtually all my interests were literary, yet once again I chose an inter-disciplinary route, returning to Yale as a Ph.D. candidate in American Studies. While I took some valuable and absorbing courses, especially ones dealing with American political and religious movements, once more I began choosing English and American literature offerings to the near exclusion of others.

At the close of one fine course –*Four Modern American Poets: Pound, Eliot, Stevens, and Williams*– Professor Louis Martz told me, "You really ought to be an English Ph.D. That, or Comparative Literature. Go where your passions lie." So, having successfully petitioned the American

Such Dancing as We Can

Studies department for an M.A., I did seek a transfer, choosing the Comp Lit option.

What was this anti-concentrative instinct in me? What is it *now*? I can't fully answer my own question. Nor did I then know that Comparative Literature would be the chief incubator of capital-T *Theory*, of which, like Flannery O'Connor, I am "constitutionally innocent."

The results have of course been predictable: even after forty-three years of teaching at rather prestigious institutions, including Yale itself (the latter half of that time, to be sure, as a putative teacher of creative writing); even after four decades-plus of trying to catch up, there still remain great gaps in my command of the English-language tradition, old-style or "open."

If you asked me to comment on eighteenth-century British literature, for example, I'd have little to say unless the conversation centered on Pope, with maybe a side comment or two on Dryden. Medieval lit for me is Chaucer, period, and a scattering of Provencal poems. Apart from the monuments of Spenser, I am comfortable with a few poems by Wyatt, with a greater number by Ben Jonson, and with the magisterial prose of *The Book of Common Prayer* (though I am familiar with that last for extra-academic reasons). And I do know *Paradise Lost*, frontwards and backwards, having been obliged to teach it in my Dartmouth years. So much for the English Renaissance and, apart from some Herbert and Donne, the sixteenth and seventeenth centuries at large.

But what of Shakespeare, you ask? Well, in addition to my lack of education in some areas, I seem to have certain bizarre dyslexias, the greatest of which involves, precisely, the Bard's work, apart from the *Sonnets* and the major tragedies.

I should say, rather, I know the major tragedies exclusive of *Hamlet,* whose intricacies escape me almost the minute I finish re-reading the play. Sitting here just now, I couldn't offer a Cliffs Notes version if you begged me. Apart from Hamlet himself and Ophelia, the play's characters run together in my mind. I can't remember, say, whether Laertes is admirable or contemptible. All I recall of Polonius is that he (I *think* it was he) hid behind a curtain for some reason. There was a play within the play, but what was its drift? And so on.

I would come to suffer acutely from these inadequacies, or rather from my effort to mask them. Fifty-plus years ago at Dartmouth, my first teaching post, for example, there was a tacit expectation of English department personnel that they spend some time in the coffee room every day. A few gimlet-eyed elders occupied certain seats there as surely as if they'd been assigned. The

Such Dancing as We Can

supposed aim of such gatherings was to promote camaraderie; the hidden agenda, however, was to sound out younger colleagues and to appraise them as worthy or otherwise. Of course, in my paranoia, I likely overestimated this darker motive...but it was there, all right.

The whole ritual felt rather Henry Jamesian in its archness and obliquity, and its threats, as I construed them, were veiled in wit. One elder, Thomas Vance, as well read a man as I have ever met, was not only a literary polymath but also uncannily able to quote immense swatches of material by heart. He would frequently do so and then, with a twinkle, assert, "Now that's pretty good (or bad)." If I showed slowness in responding, he would sit back and muse, "Perhaps you don't agree"– whereupon I scrambled to offer my acquiescence, lest he query me further on my delinquent taste.

In fact, Tom soon became one of the very few senior associates to encourage me in my early poetic efforts, and he shortly proved a real friend. Once we established these closer relations, I admitted to him that my memory of our early dialogue consisted principally of my saying, "Why, no, Tom, I don't think I *have* read that."

How well I remember the dread I tasted as I mounted the stairs of Sanborn House after a morning class. It didn't matter if my oversight of a particular session had been vibrant. Such a petty triumph provided no solace; my stomach progressively contracted with every step.

Eventually, my modest successes as a writer of poetry, first and foremost, but also of fiction, personal essays, and even a couple volumes of non-specialistic criticism mollified some of my anxieties. Both as author and as founding editor of an admired literary quarterly, I also knew great quantities of material of which those elders had been ignorant– particularly poetry after the Moderns. In many cases, they excused their unawareness by mocking the work of most living writers as trivial, unless, that is, they happened to be British; but I took some small satisfaction in sensing their embarrassment when I raised the name, say, of Adrienne Rich, though of course their shame must have been mild, compared to what mine had been at its severest.

Let me go back to that corny song from which I quoted at the outset.

Wait. Did I just call it corny? This goes to show that, despite what I'll claim henceforth, I harbor more than a touch of the old gut-clenching fear: *I am not smart or sophisticated enough.* That is, my choice of that very adjective shows how conditioned I became over time either to hiding certain enthusiasms that sprang to mind or to ironizing them. I was after all exposed for quite a long while to the edicts of trained excellence.

My purpose in composing these thoughts is to purge such reactions.

Now I know that "She Loved a Lot in Her Time," George Jones's tribute to his mother Clara, is not great poetry, that its hold on my heart and soul derives primarily from the late singer's exquisite capacity to vocalize emotion. (Someone once said that Jones could sing the phone book and make a grownup cry.) But by God, that hold on heart and soul is strong, and I mean to stop apologizing for it.

No more masks, say I, stealing the title of Bass and Howe's brilliant feminist anthology of the seventies.

As I look back on where I was as a mere kid, on what happened, and on where I am at this very long-deferred moment, certain heroes shine in memory. Richard Hugo, a masterful poet whose reputation, unlike Erwin Fiske's, is now in what I hope to be temporary eclipse, proved a generous mentor when I decided that my ambitions were more poetic than scholarly. A *lot* more.

I once mailed Dick a poem, along with a note in which I worried lest it be, precisely, corny. He had some criticisms, needless to say. I do not remember what they were. What I do remember is the last sentence of his reply: "If you aren't risking corn, well, you're not even in the ballgame."

I likewise recall something Maxine Kumin said to me in the middle seventies after a Bread Loaf lecture that had confused us both. The talk was delivered by what I suppose was a "postmodern" poet ahead of his time. Irony, verging on nihilism from my perspective, was at its core; that much we did understand. Maxine sighed, and told me that, for her money anyhow, "Poetry is strong feeling presented in the best language a person can find to render it. Period." Reductive? Well yes, as Maxine well knew. But that simplistic notion of a poem (or, in the case in point, a song) comes much closer to what I am looking for in life and art than does supercilious cool.

Both Hugo and Kumin helped set me on the path I have pursued as a poet myself, and as I've aged, that path has been widened by predilections I've had all along but have been hesitant to acknowledge, much less to exhibit.

Truth is, I know now, as I did from the start of my idiosyncratic academic career, all manner of vital things that those elder dons had no idea of, including a great range of American vernacular music, from the bluegrass tradition originating with Bill Monroe, to Hank Williams,

Such Dancing as We Can

Buck Owens, Dolly Parton, Merle Haggard, Tami Wynette, Waylon Jennings, Willie Nelson— on and on. I'm likewise deeply attuned to the twelve-bar triumphs of the great Delta bluesmen and their scions in r&b and Motown and soul. I'm quite conversant with the blues-derived music of great American jazz artists too, especially masters from the late bop era of Monk, Mingus, Rollins, Roach, Davis, and the glorious rest.

It's about time I got unabashed about such knowledge, and to worry a lot less about my abiding ignorance of certain other creative efforts. No need to rehearse the dissimulation I practiced on my high school music teacher, say, a wonderful instructor at that, but one contemptuous of anything other than what he described as "true music." Quite daringly by community standards, for example, he introduced me to Webern, Berg, and Stockhausen, to whom I made a show of pledging allegiance, even if in all truth serial music struck me –and still does– as simply unpleasant, especially compared, for example, to the lyrical splendors of Bobby Bland, Etta James, or Ray Charles. I'd as soon have shown my private diaries to Mr. C. as reveal that side of my tastes. But things have changed. Better late than never.

Whatever has become of me as man and author, it took all the omissions and inclusions, deceptions and candors, steps and missteps, first and second thoughts that I have dimly presented here to make me that man and author. Having no choice this late in the game, I'm trying to celebrate the whole bewildering process, to acknowledge that in *all* my pursuits, Sam Cook has been more important to me, for instance, than Sam Johnson– and to feel no shame whatever in saying so.

So now, as the saw goes, I seem set in my ways. I'm aware that there can be real costs involved. There are too many historical instances of old men and women who have not "gotten it," who have taken bumptious pride in missing the point, too many for me to believe myself immune from such blindness. My own children sneer when I admit, say, that what the rappers produce is neither music nor poetry to my ear, and, given that those children are if anything brighter than I am, no, I don't have much reason to doubt I'm overlooking something. So be it.

If, to choose another example, I decided to read the poems of the late John Ashbery (which I quite scrupulously do *not* do anymore), and if I concluded that there must be some clever inside joke going on there that gets by me but is clear to the intelligentsia; if I find the man's poetry to be so much gibberish, find it inscrutable (like the kindred and unreadable critical theory that has overtaken what used to be literature departments)– if I

Such Dancing as We Can

find his opus to have played a part in spawning a mode of verse whose principal objective appears to be opacity: well, I am done with feeling abashed on that account.

Nolo contendere. I don't care what the smart people think anymore.

There, that wasn't so hard, was it?

Hey, I feel pretty good.

Sydney Lea

REUNION

Every year just after Memorial Day, when the blackflies are at their cruelest, I take a Maine fishing trip with my brother Jake, his twin daughters, my two sons and one of my daughters. It's topwater angling for smallmouth bass, which, while they guard their spawning beds, turn as vicious as those blackflies. They doubtless strike our Muddlers and poppers more out of anger than hunger.

We are short on canoes for such a company, so we need to hire a guide or two, one of whom I've known since I was more or less a kid. I've encountered hundreds of other professional outdoorsmen and -women over the decades, but none has equaled him for savvy. As my brother once remarked, "Every trip with him, land or water, is a nature lesson." I cherish this man's friendship.

I don't thrill to the fight of the smallmouths as I once did, but the rest of the outing is dearer to me than ever. Come March, I start looking forward to seeing that local friend and so many of our clan in one dear place. Even apart from the wonderful human connections, there would be a lot to savor, like the craftsmanship that goes into the locally made motor canoes: their beautiful ash thwarts and ribs; their cedar hulls; their transoms, often wrought from exotic mahogany.

Such Dancing as We Can

That's not even to mention the lakes themselves. Very little water exists in North America or anywhere else these days that's as clear as theirs. An equal marvel: we can drink from each lake. I daydream of their very offshore rocks, glacial erratics that provide good fish cover, and of their surroundings woods, which crowd the waters right down to the sand with softwood growth as thick as hair. The pickerelweed in the shallows, not yet quite in bloom, nonetheless shows a hint of the lavender to come. There are other splendors, of course: moose, deer, osprey, eagle, beaver, mink, otter– that list is also a long one. Our place in Vermont, so different topographically, is just as lovely in its different way, and yet my escapes to this other landscape, which I've made since 1953, always feel like blessings.

The spring of 2022, however, saw COVID spiking in that part of the world. The only medical facility anywhere nearby is a minuscule clinic. Jake and I, both oldsters now, , decided to call the trip off.

But soon all the kids reminded us that they'd made arrangements, some at great effort, to get time away from work, and, more important, that the family reunion is always more important than the bass fishing anyhow. So why not test for COVID before arrival, then go to our camp just for the company? After all, we'd be in a remote place, removed even from the very sparse local populace.

We did bring our rods… which stayed in their cases. Stories by the score were pulled out instead, many poking affectionate fun at one or more of our gang, especially its older members. Those anecdotes came as relentlessly as the laughter. We took turns preparing meals, and the food was superb as well. Above all, the sense of family continuity affected everyone, particularly us brothers, the tribal elders now, however sudden and shocking that seems to us both.

And again, it was more than merely significant that our gathering evolved in a place where the sunsets over the lake were as stunning as ever, where the freshness of the prevailing northwest wind and the air's evergreen scent seemed tonic, where something like the dive of a fish hawk or the exuberant leap of a salmon proved a priceless spectacle. This list could likewise go on and on.

Now I'm not at all some deluded back-to-the-Paleolithic type. Nor will I let myself wax too sentimental about nature's "harmony," as some too easily do. They must never have seen the likes of what I saw one spring from my turkey blind: a coyote eating a young snowshoe hare alive, the poor thing shrieking until it couldn't.

Such Dancing as We Can

For all of that, our non-fishing trip did make me more vividly aware than ever that, beyond a world in which our significant encounters increasingly come by way of a screen, there lies a wider and more venerable one. Our gathering provided things that transcend the technologies: it revealed the importance of binding affections, and it did so in a place that reminded us how impoverished our distinction between capital-N Nature and human nature can be.

Sydney Lea

EPILOGUE: MATURITY

Before long, this, unlike the essay preceding– will be chiefly a fisherman's tale, but I'm somehow moved to begin with a digression. I seem to do that more and more these days. A friend in Maine, a guide who sits with me on the board of the local land trust, was once interviewed by a podcaster, one of whose questions was about how it felt to be a colleague of Vermont's poet laureate, which I was honored to be at the time.

That friend replied, "Well, the stories can be a little longer than a lot I hear."

Well, small surprise, things coming at me from many directions nowadays, especially when I wake up at 3 a.m. In fact, they often arrive in such supply that they keep me from sleep for hours. My recounting some of them later along is involuntary, like some people's compulsion to sneeze in a field of ragweed.

Apart from family memories, I primarily summon old sporting experiences. I was so avid for so many years that at times I look back on my younger self as someone nearly exotic.

I can far too frequently and despairingly compare what I'm able to do at my current age to what I could do from

Such Dancing as We Can

the early sixties right into the two thousand aughts. If today I find myself pretty tuckered out after a couple of hours of hunting grouse, say, in the thick New England brush, I am inevitably taken by surprise. I know how absurd that is. I also know I'm not alone. I add this as diagnosis, not excuse, but I'm not the only one to indulge in such silliness, at least not among people of my gender. (My experience indicates that women are simply saner about such matters… no, about everything.)

I'm retired now, but for four decades I was a college professor. In those days, I would arrange my schedule so as to wade or drift countless rivers and lakes. I sought often to teach the short summer term, in which I could hold classes and office hours during the day and still reach one of three nearby rivers in time for evening hatches.

Now most of my fly angling transpired in northern New England, but fishing took me as well across the Atlantic to Spain (salmon), to France and Scotland (trout) and on this side of the ocean to Canada (salmon), Alaska (huge rainbows), Cape Cod (stripers and blues), irrigation canals in south Florida (freshwater tarpon) and trout streams in Arkansas, Pennsylvania, New York, Washington, California, Colorado, Connecticut, Wyoming, Idaho and above all Montana.

I began my fishing career, however, well before I picked up a fly rod. My parents often rented a cottage on the New Jersey shore, where I would dangle bait off piers, dreaming of a stray snapper blue, but happy with any one of the saltwater breams. Too often I had to settle for a sea robin or skate, yet despite such frustrations, my excitement, especially if the catch would be something I could bring home for the table, almost equaled what I'd later feel when the browns started rising on a slick.

I will return to these Jersey recollections before I'm through.

Although these days I now and then fish for bass and trout from boats, I don't wade, my balance having simply gotten too unreliable. I do still go after the upland birds in some measure, but if I trip or slide —and Lord knows I do—at least I'm not going to be washed away by bossy water.

For all that may be lost to me, however, I have small grounds for complaint. As I've iterated throughout this book, mine has been a good life in almost every way imaginable. By and large I've also enjoyed good health, financial security, professional gratification and all the outdoor episodes implanted so vividly in a mind that's still largely functional. Do my sporting endeavors tend now to be ones I arrive at by reminiscence? Well, that's to

Such Dancing as We Can

be expected. It does no good to lament that reality, though yes, now and then I do, for all the fruitless energy it wastes.

Looking back on my sporting career, I see many a highlight, a few low ones as well, and even some miracles– for example this one. On Colorado's Crystal River, I once set my streamer's hook in a brown trout big and strong enough that I had no choice but to move with him as he ran downstream in the brawling current. When I arrived at a sheer slate bank and couldn't follow anymore, I simply jumped in, held my rod high, and rode the rips thirty yards or so until I could find my feet. Yes, miracles: first, that I'm here to talk about such madness (and I could recount a litany of further all but equally mad adventures); second, that my trout was still on! I knocked his head –unlike now, back then I killed a big fish when I netted one– so I could take him back. I wanted to show my friends and, crucially, to tell the tale of hauling him in.

I see everything as clearly today as I did almost sixty years ago: that emerald valley, that white stretch of river, those sublime, golden mountains in the distance, and above all the trout itself– gorgeous, all spangled halo and gilded skin, though for some reason one of his pectoral fins was missing.

Sydney Lea

Likely the story I told when I showed up soaking wet at our camp *was*, as my guide friend would later suggest, longer than many.

Another time, well after dark, I fooled a brown in a river whose name I've forgotten, though I know it was near Pau in France's low Pyrenees. The fish, having dived into a blowdown on the far bank, immediately snapped the leader. (6x tippets were a lot more fragile fifty-five years ago than they are today.) I cursed, my passions those of a willful young man whose competitiveness with his quarry could be nigh catastrophic, as the earlier incident on the Crystal had shown.

I thought, *I'm done, damn it all.* The hour had gotten too late to keep casting. I'd need to use a flashlight merely to find my way back to the road where I'd left my motorcycle. As I turned to leave, however, I suddenly heard a different sound above the stream's lisp, one coming, precisely, from the brush pile where my trout had broken off. Wading over, I shone a beam on the water.

There was my brown– not a trophy, to be sure, but a marvel indeed. He'd wrapped some seven or eight inches of leader around a slender branch, lithe enough to play him since the moment he broke me off.

Such Dancing as We Can

Later, the cook at my *pension,* and eternal thanks to her, prepared the trout in the classic *almondine* fashion, well after the few other guests had had their dinners. I haven't tasted anything better since.

Again, it's the physical scene that stays with me: the very last of the alpenglow evanescing from the near mountains, the sudden, startling cries from some nearby night bird whose identity I have never been able to discover, the ghostly glimmer of the chalk cliffs, the sautéed trout on a pewter dish, which that generous cook laid on a claret-spotted tablecloth.

On another day, I killed a couple of more or less bragging-size fish on the White River in Vermont and stuck them into my canvas creel. I happened to turn around at one point just in time to see a mink dragging the bag away. The sun on the critter's back, the curious little coughing sound he made as I shooed him away, the grace of his speedy underwater flight: these too are as vivid in memory as they were when I actually witnessed them.

You can see the way my fancy works. I have loved both fish and game not least for where I found it. I miss being there (or multiple theres), but in my saner moments, I recognize how lucky I am that I have those places to fetch back.

Sydney Lea

Like anyone fortunate enough to live a long time, of course, I have known some deep pains: the loss of my wonderful father much too young, of my poor younger brother dropped by an aneurysm in his thirties, of a cherished brother-in-law taken by cancer in his fifties. Other treasured men and women have died or lost their cognitive faculties since. On the other hand, I don't look back on stultifying factory or farm labor, on grueling poverty, on military terrors, what have you, and I am scarcely lacking in outdoor adventures now, no matter I'd have sneered at some of them in the times I bring to mind.

One hears of people going into second childhood, and I too am old enough now for re-entry. As I pledged at the outset, it's those childhood moments of dapping for fish on the New Jersey shore to which I return, at least obliquely, as I finish these reflections, even though it's not truly *my* childhood to which I revert in my later years. I can joyously share others' youthful enthusiasms. Their excitement over a primitive mode of angling recalls for me those early mornings on mid-Atlantic wharves when, before my parents left their beds, before the dank summer heat blanketed everything, I dropped a line into the brine and dreamed of hooking something beyond my dreams.

Such Dancing as We Can

All of which brings me to this: not so terribly long ago, my wife, who wasn't raised in a fishing family, decided that she wanted to do more than merely fish; she wanted to try her hand at catching one of the very few species that lie beyond my catch-and-release strictures: the delicious white perch.

Our Maine camp sits by a lake –don't ask where it is—on which engines are not permitted. It provides no public launch, and hauling motorless boat or canoe through the heavy woods to the water is too daunting for most. I scarcely blame them. There are only five other dwellings around us, all on one shore. Each is seasonal, and almost none of their owners visits with the regularity we do in our retirement. Ours therefore often feels like a private lake, a place of calm and, apart from loons' cries and eagles' screams, of extraordinary quiet.

But my *internal* excitement was loud the first time I took my wife to one of the perch holes. We'd recently bought a wonderful watercraft from Adirondack Guide Boat, whose shop is located not far from us. We chose what its makers call the Vermont Fishing Dory, which can be rowed backwards or forwards, and although it's very light, offers exceptional stability. It's ideal for the sort of pan fishing I speak of, though it would also make a fine drift boat. It'd be excellent for trolling as well for those who enjoy that sort of angling, as I do not; it rows that easily and swiftly.

I was keen both to try our new guide boat and to behold my wife reeling in supper. I suppose I could mope about watching her spinning rod bend with a big perch (they grow up to a pound and a half in our secret spot) and feeling a kindred animation to behold a big trout sipping my dry used to do. I choose, rather, to celebrate the fact that this sort of ultra-basic angling is available to me now, when my physical prowess is so much less available than once, though in fact I'm generally content to bait my spouse's hook and net her catch.

I likewise greatly look forward to introducing two further grandchildren, seven and four, to the spots that hold white perch.

I should perhaps have mentioned that I'm curiously animated too by setting my trap for the minnows we use on those perch. I delight in a good haul, just as I delight in experimenting with bait for them, much as I used to do in sorting through trout flies. Black-nosed dace seem especially fond of dog biscuits, which have the advantage of holding up well, and the more fragile butt ends of baguettes, but I have tried everything from pasta to peanut butter, the latter representing the only real bust I've experienced.

Such Dancing as We Can

As with all my most memorable outdoor moments in the past, every successful trip to the perch hole lodges itself not least because of the context in which it takes place. On a fair day, the sky never looks so blue; the clouds are sharp-edged; as they cross the sun, it lights them like lanterns from within; the evergreen woods that crowd every stone beach are almost black with their own density; loons patrol our periphery, hoping for a minnow coughed up by a fish as my wife cranks it in, the shine of those Paleolithic birds' plumage downright thrilling.

And the evening meal on our screened-in porch enchants us at least equally. The food is exquisite, and an indescribable sunset glow suffuses the eastern shore. The closer that glow comes to its death, the more beautiful it becomes.

Sydney Lea

ACKNOWLEDGMENTS

I owe significant debts, though some of my benefactors may not even know just *how* significant, to Steven Harvey, Bruce Richards, Joe Mackall, Robert Nazarene, Fleda Brown, DeWitt Henry, Paula Deitz, Ron Koury, Stephen Bluestone, Dinty Moore, Tony Whedon, Michael Simms, Marjan Strojan, Ron Slate, and above all my marvelous editor at The Humble Essayist Press, Kathryn Winograd. As my dedication indicates, I'll always feel gratitude to the late Stephen Arkin, soul mate and abundantly helpful critic for almost sixty years, and life would scarcely be the blessing it is without my wife Robin Barone, our five children, and seven grandchildren.

I would like to thank the editors of the following journals, in which some of these essays originally appeared, sometimes in slightly and sometimes in radically different forms:

Agni, Atticus Review, Brevity, Eclectica, Expanded Field (The Netherlands), *The American Journal of Poetry, bioStories, Connotation, Epoch Press Literary Journal (U.K.), Fourth Genre, The Gettysburg Review, Gray's Sporting Journal, The Hudson Review, JAMA (The Journal of the American Medical Association), Juxtaprose, Main Street Rag, Nadwah, New Ohio Review, Northern Woodlands, The Notre Dame Review, Numéro Cinq, Oldster Magazine, On the Seawall, Pensive, Pratik,*

Such Dancing as We Can

Querencia Press, River Teeth, Sport Literate, Stymie, The Commuter, The Tahoma Literary Review, upstreet, The Vermont Almanac, Vox Populi, The Woven Tale.

The following essays first appeared in *What's the Story?* (Green Writers Press, Brattleboro, VT, 2012): *American Dream, Storytelling at the Res, Short Sad Story, Forgiveness, Mrs. Ragnetti and the Spider, The Couple at the Free Pile, One More Eulogy*

Sydney Lea

STUDY GUIDE

1. Perhaps because Lea is at heart a poet, his essays are very segmented and often end abruptly, often with only an image for a "conclusion." As Lea frequently points out, often small occurrences or observations jolt him back into deep memories of the past. Lea doesn't always explain the connection between the image and the memories. One example is in The Cardinal, The Cops, and The Say-Hey Kid , which begins and ends with a cardinal that Lea finds. The ending of this essay is rather shocking: the cardinal dead, Lea throws its "brilliant body" into a wood stove and describes the cardinal's body as "lighter than air." How does this image work with an essay in which Lea touches on the racism he remembers from his childhood? How do we reconcile the two? What other essays end with an image and how do you "read" them?

2. For a personal memoir in essays, Lea's book is filled with the stories of many other people: people he grew up with, people he met, people he heard about, people he loved. Choose some of your favorite "other" characters in the book. What do these characters add to Lea's personal story? What lessons does Lea learn from these characters as he contemplates the eightieth year of his life?

3. Lea brings up miracles and blessings throughout this collection as he contemplates his life. Does the book belong in the genre of books on faith and spirituality? If so, what kind of spirituality is at the center of Lea's faith?

4. Thanatophobia is the fear of oncoming death. Lea's later essays in the collection recount the various debilitating ailments, mishaps, and deaths of those Lea has known through the years. Some might imagine that such a focus would make Such Dancing As We Can a depressing book to read. But the argument could be made that despite, or even because of this focus, the book is not disheartened and that, ultimately, Lea comes to terms with those stories directly and indirectly. Is this book about one's man's fear of death? Or not? If not, how is any thanatophobia tamed?

5. Lea often quotes from other writers, either through epigraphs at the start of essays or in the middle of essays. Those quotations bring in other voices to his essays and create another layer to his prose. Choose a couple of instances where Lea has brought in the words of another and talk about how such borrowings affect Lea's stories. What might the essays lose without these other voices?

6. The writer Alexander Chee writes in her introduction to The Best American Essays that during the years of Covid, when she was trying to deal with the debilitation of an entire world and her own family, she lost faith in what writing could or could not do, doubting its ability to "improve anything between people." She doubted "especially the idea that writing could or should create empathy." Do these essays of Lea's serve as a counter-argument or at least a salve to such a crisis of faith in writing? If so, how?

Made in United States
North Haven, CT
19 January 2024